Patchwork and Quilting
Book Number 3

Twenty seven projects by Kaffe Fassett • Roberta Horton
Liza Prior Lucy • Sandy Donabed • Kim Hargreaves
Pauline Smith • Brandon Mably

A WESTMINSTER PRODUCTION

First Published in Great Britain in 2001 by
Rowan Yarns
Green Lane Mill
Holmfirth
West Yorkshire
England
HD9 2DX

Copyright Rowan Yarns 2001

Published in the U. S. A. by
Westminster Fibers Inc.
5 Northern Boulevard,
Amherst,
New Hampshire 03031
U.S.A.

Editor and text: Jane Bolsover
Art Director: Kim Hargreaves
Patchwork Designs: Kaffe Fassett, Liza Prior Lucy, Pauline Smith,
Kim Hargreaves, Roberta Horton, Sandra Townsend Donabed and Brandon Mably
Quilters: Judy Irish
Photographer: Joey Toller
Design layout: Les Dunford
Illustrations: Siriol Clarry
Sub Editor: Natalie Minnis
Feature: Linda Parkhouse
Machine thread: Drima and Sylko in UK, Coats Dual Duty Polyester USA

American Congress Library
Westminster Fibers
Patchwork and Quilting
IBSN 0-9672985-2-0

Colour reproduction by Chroma Graphics (Overseas) Pte. Ltd
Printed and bound in Singapore by KHL Printing Co. Pte. Ltd.

CONTENTS

INTRODUCTION

What a terrific response we got from our last *Patchwork and Quilting* book. During an exhibition earlier this year, someone stopped me to say, 'Book Number 2 was a 250 percent improvement on the first book - how can you possibly do that again?' So I'm thrilled to bring you *Patchwork and Quilting Book Number 3*, which I feel has been improved yet again!

This year we have an even greater selection of projects - 27 in total - to suit all skill levels. Once more Kaffe Fassett has produced nine wonderful new designs for this year's book, along with Kim Hargreaves, Liza Prior Lucy and Pauline Smith. In addition, we are thrilled to have quilts especially designed for this year's book by Sandra Townsend Donabed, Brandon Mably and world-renowned artist Roberta Horton.

Roberta, a Californian, has been teaching quiltmaking since 1972 and is particularly interested in the Amish influences on quilt design. Linda Parkhouse went to meet Roberta in America, to talk about her passion for quilts and the Amish community. Turn to page 77 to find this brand new section, which we very much hope you'll enjoy reading.

And what wonderful new fabrics do we have for you this year? Well the Rowan range just keeps growing. I'm sure you won't be able to resist the new shot cottons with names like watermelon, sunshine, rosy and custard. Then there's the Rowan Stripes, a great new collection of two-coloured stripes in the beautiful soft faded colour palette of the shot cottons. Take a look at Kaffe's Sail Away quilt on page 28, to see how fabulous these look.

Finally, this year's book is in full colour all the way through, including the Patchwork know-how section and the templates, which should make it much easier to trace them off.

All that remains is for me to wish you many hours of fun and happy quilting!

Jane Bolsover.

Jane Bolsover, Editor

SEA BREEZE

Eight projects in a soft faded palette, reminiscent of days gone by –
fabrics aged and faded by the sun – think candy floss, ice-cream,
summer flowers and driftwood tones

Pale Bob's Your Uncle
by Kaffe Fassett
Instructions on page 6

Pale Bob's Your Uncle

KAFFE FASSETT

For this baby quilt, Kaffe wanted to design a joyful candy-coloured arrangement of patches. Notice how the placement of the various fabric colours and prints in the design create an over and under effect, rather like weaving. This is very different from the dark version of this quilt (see page 50), where the fabric placements make the blocks appear as squares.

SIZE OF QUILT

The finished quilt will measure approximately 42in x 50½in (107cm x 128cm).

MATERIALS

Patchwork fabrics:
GP 01-BW: ⅛yd (15cm) or 1FQ
GP 01-PK: ⅛yd (15cm) or 1FQ
GP 02-L: ⅛yd (15cm) or 1FQ
GP 02-C: ⅛yd (15cm) or 1FQ
GP 03-S: ⅛yd (15cm) or 1FQ
GP 06-C: ¼yd (23cm) or 1FQ
GP 06-S: ⅛yd (15cm) or 1FQ
GP 06-P: ⅛yd (15cm) or 1FQ
GP 06-L: ⅛yd (15cm) or 1FQ
GP 07-C: ⅛yd (15cm) or 1FQ
GP 07-L: ⅛yd (15cm) or 1FQ
GP 07-S: ⅛yd (15cm) or 1FQ
GP 07-P: ⅛yd (15cm) or 1FQ
GP 08-L: ⅛yd (15cm) or 1FQ
GP 08-C: ¼yd (23cm) or 1FQ
GP 08-S: See border corners
OS 02: ½yd (45cm) or 2 FQ

Outer borders:
GP 02-S: ⅔yd (60cm)

Border corners:
GP 08-S: ¼yd (23cm) or 1FQ

Backing:
GP 04-P: 1⅔yd (1.5m)

Bias binding:
BWS 01: ¼yd (23cm).

Batting:
48in x 56in (122cm x 142cm)

Quilting thread:
Toning machine quilting thread.

PATCH SHAPES

The quilt centre is made from one small square patch (template S) and a rectangle (template T). The quilt centre is bordered

Templates

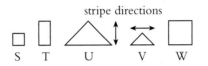

S   T   U   V   W

by large triangles (template U), with small triangles at the corners (template V). There are straight outer borders, with a large square at each corner (template W). See pages 82, 83 and 84 for templates.

CUTTING OUT

Template S: Cut 2½in- (6.5cm-) wide strips across width of fabric. Each strip will give you 18 patches per 45in- (114cm-) wide fabric, or 8 per FQ (see page 94). Cut 32 in GP 06-C.
Template T: Cut 8 in GP 01-PK, GP 01-BW (W.S), GP 02-L, GP 02-C, GP 03-S (W.S), GP 06-S, GP 06-P, GP 06-L, GP 07-L (W.S), GP 07-S (W.S), GP 07-C (W.S), GP 07-P, GP 08-L and GP 08-S. Cut 16 in GP 08-C.
Template U: Cut 14 in OS 02.
Template V: Cut 8 in OS 02.
Template W: Cut 4 in GP 08-S.
Outer borders:
Cut 2 side borders 4½in x 34½in (11.5cm x 87.5cm) and 2 end borders 4½in x 43in (11.5cm x 109cm) in GP 02-S.
Backing:
Cut 1 piece 45in x 56in (114cm x 142cm) in GP 04-P.
Bias binding:
Cut 5¼yds (4.75m) of bias binding 2¼in- (6cm-) wide from BWS 01.

MAKING THE BLOCKS

Using a ¼in (6mm) seam allowance make up 32 blocks, using the block and quilt

assembly diagrams as a guide and stitch between the dots only. When inserting the last patch into each block, use the inset seam technique (see page 96).

Block assembly

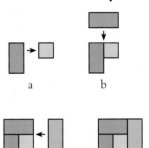

a   b

c   d

ASSEMBLING THE BLOCKS

Arrange the 32 blocks and 14 large triangles into 8 diagonal rows following the quilt assembly diagram. Using a ¼in (6mm) seam allowance, join the blocks together into rows, then join the rows together to form the top. Join 2 small triangles together for each corner of the quilt centre and stitch to the corners.

MAKING THE OUTER BORDERS

Using a ¼in (6mm) seam allowance, attach the 2 side borders to the quilt edges. Join a corner square (template W) to each end of the end borders and attach to the quilt edges.

FINISHING THE QUILT

Press the assembled quilt top. Layer the quilt top, batting and backing, and baste together (see pages 98 and 99).

Quilt assembly

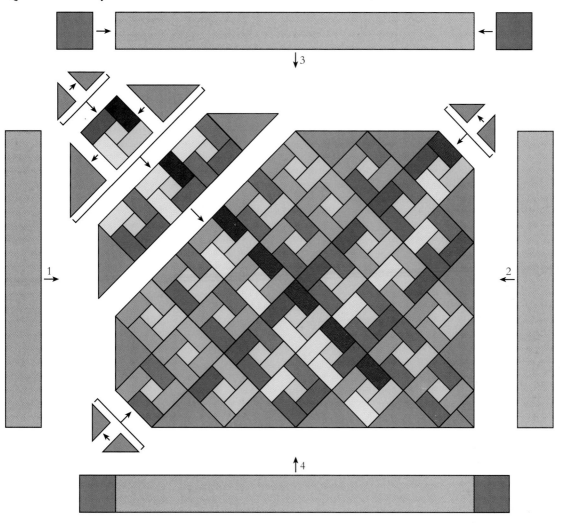

key

blocks

■ = GP 07-C(WS)	■ = GP 01-BW(WS)	■ = GP 02-L
■ = GP 07-P	■ = GP 07-L(WS)	■ = GP 07-S(WS)
■ = GP 06-S	■ = GP 08-L	■ = GP 06-P
■ = GP 03-S(WS)	■ = GP 08-C	■ = GP 06-L
■ = GP 02-C	■ = GP 08-S	■ = GP 01-PK

block centres

■ = GP 06-C

outer triangles

■ = OS 02

borders

■ = GP 02-S

■ = GP 08-S

Quilting

Using the quilting diagram, right, as a guide, free-motion quilt the quilt centre in a very random fashion working across each row of blocks at a time. Free-motion quilt around the outer borders in the same manner.

Trim the quilt edges and attach the binding (see page 99).

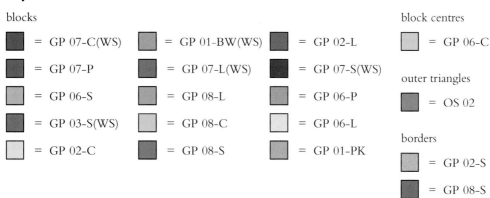
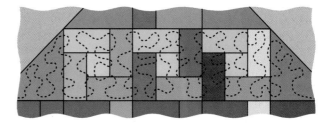

Pale Pin Wheels

KAFFE FASSETT

This particular quilt is a design that Kaffe produced in the past for his *Passionate Patchwork* book. Being renowned for his amazing talent for combining colours, he wanted to take the design a step further and experiment to see what a softer pastel version would be like. This beautifully quilted patchwork is the result.

SIZE OF QUILT

The finished quilt will measure approximately 50in x 50in (127cm x 127cm).

MATERIALS

Patchwork fabrics:
GP 02-L: ¼yd (23cm) or 1FQ
GP 02-P: ¼yd (23cm) or 1FQ
GP 02-CT: ¼yd (23cm) or 1FQ
GP 03-P: ¼yd (23cm) or 1FQ
GP 04-P: See backing
GP 06-P: ¼yd (23cm) or 1FQ
GP 07-P: ¼yd (23cm) or 1FQ
GP 08-L: ¼yd (23cm) or 1FQ
GP 08-C: ¼yd (23cm) or 1FQ
SC 28: 1⅓yds (1.2m) or 6FQ

Backing:
GP 04-P: 2⅔yds (2.4m)

Bias binding:
RS 05: ¼yd (23cm)

Batting:
56in x 56in (142cm x 142cm)

Quilting thread:
Toning machine quilting thread

Templates

HH   II

PATCH SHAPES

The quilt top is made from 2 sizes of pin wheel. The small pin wheels are made from 1 small triangle (template II) and the large from a large triangle (template HH). See page 87 and 88 for templates.

CUTTING OUT

Template II: Cut 3⅜in- (8.5cm-) wide strips across width of fabric. Each strip will give you 26 patches per 45in- (114cm-) wide fabric, or 12 per FQ (see page 94).
Cut 128 in SC 28. Cut 8 in GP 02-P, GP 03-P and GP 06-P, 12 in GP 08-L, 16 in GP 04-P and GP 07-P, 20 in GP 02-L, GP 02-CT and GP 08-C.

Template HH: Cut 5⅞in- (15cm-) wide strips across width of fabric. Each strip will give you 14 patches per 45in- (114cm-) wide fabric, or 6 per FQ (see page 94).
Cut 68 in SC 28. Cut 4 in GP 04-P and GP 06-P; 8 in GP 02-P, GP 02-L, GP 02-CT, GP 03-P, GP 07-P and GP 08-C; 12 in GP 08-L.

Backing:
Cut 1 piece 45in x 56in (114cm x 142cm) and 2 pieces 12in x 28¼in (30.5cm x 72cm) in GP 04-P.

Bias binding:
Cut 5⅔yds (5.1m) of bias binding 2½- (6.5cm-) wide from RS 05.

MAKING THE PIN WHEEL UNITS

Using a ¼in (6mm) seam allowance, make up 17 large pin wheel units and 32 small pin wheel units, following the unit assembly diagrams shown top right.

MAKING THE SMALL PIN WHEEL BLOCKS

Using a ¼in (6mm) seam allowance, assemble 8 pin wheel blocks, using the small block assembly diagram, see right, and quilt assembly diagrams as a guide, see page 10.

Unit assembly

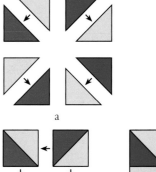

a

b   c

Small block assembly

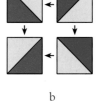

a

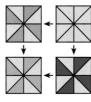

b

ASSEMBLING THE BLOCKS

Using the quilt assembly diagram as a guide (see page 10), arrange the centre row of 2 small pin wheel blocks with 1 large pin wheel unit in between. Using a ¼in (6mm) seam allowance, join the

8

Quilt assembly

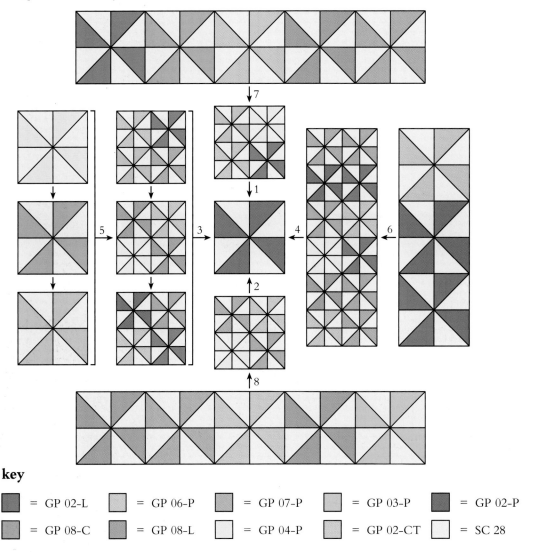

key

■ = GP 02-L	■ = GP 06-P	■ = GP 07-P	■ = GP 03-P	■ = GP 02-P	
■ = GP 08-C	■ = GP 08-L	□ = GP 04-P	■ = GP 02-CT	□ = SC 28	

blocks and unit into a row. Following the numbered order on the quilt assembly diagram, arrange 2 rows of 3 small pin wheel blocks and stitch together. Join to each side of the central row. Arrange 2 rows of 3 large pin wheel units, stitch together to form 2 rows, and join to each side of the quilt. Finally arrange 2 rows of 5 large pin wheel units, join units together and stitch to the remaining sides.

FINISHING THE QUILT

Press the assembled quilt top. Seam the 3 backing pieces of fabric together with a⅜in (1cm) seam allowance to form one large piece approximately 56in x 56in (142cm x 142cm).

Layer the quilt top, batting and backing, and baste together (see page 98).

Using a toning thread, machine quilt each small pin wheel unit in the shape of a snail shell, starting and finishing each time,

Quilting large pinwheel units   **Quilting small pinwheel units**

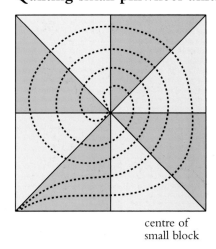

centre of
large block

centre of
small block

at the centre of the pin wheel block (see quilting diagram). Quilt each quarter section of the large pin wheel units in

the same manner (see quilting diagram). Trim the quilt edges and attach the binding (see page 99).

10

Mary Mary
by Pauline Smith
Instructions on page 12

Mary Mary

PAULINE SMITH

★★

Pauline was inspired to make this brightly coloured quilt with naive appliquéd flowers, after receiving a drawing from her 5-year-old niece. The design is very stylized - almost like a printed textile - but easy to construct being made mainly from large plain blocks. It is a simple project to adapt into a small cot quilt, or a larger double bed quilt, with the addition or subtraction of extra rows.

SIZE OF QUILT

The finished quilt will measure approximately 58in x 79in (147cm x 200cm).

MATERIALS

Patchwork and appliqué fabrics:
SC 03: ½yd (45cm) or 2FQ
SC 07: ½yd (45cm) or 2FQ
SC 08: see corner squares
SC 09: ½yd (45cm) or 2FQ
SC 12: ⅓yd (30cm) or 1FQ
SC 14: ½yd (45cm) or 2FQ
SC 20: ⅓yd (30cm) or 1FQ
SC 21: see borders
SC 26: ¼yd (23cm) or 1FQ
SC 27: ¼yd (23cm) or 1FQ
BWS 01: ⅔yd (60cm) or 4FQ
RS 03: ¼yd (23cm) or 1FQ
Borders:
SC 21: 1yd (90cm)
Corner squares:
SC 08: ½yd (45cm) or 1FQ
Backing:
NC 03: 4⅛yd (3.8m)
Straight cut binding:
NC 03: see backing.
Batting:
64in x 85in (153cm x 216cm)
Quilting thread:
Toning machine quilting thread.

PATCH SHAPES

The quilt centre is made up of five different rows A, B, C, D and E. Each row is made up of plain blocks pieced together with one pieced strip block (excluding row E).
Row A is made from one square appliquéd block, one rectangular appliquéd block (see page 82 for appliqué templates), one small rectangular block and a pieced block. The pieced block is made from three tiny squares (template A), three medium sized rectangles (template B), one long strip (template C), one small rectangle (template D) and one long thicker strip (template E). See page 81 for templates.
Row B is made from one large rectangle, one medium rectangle, one small rectangle and one pieced block. The pieced block is made from seven strips (template F). See page 81 for template.
Row C is made from one large rectangular appliquéd block (see page 82 for appliqué templates), one small rectangular block and one pieced block. The pieced block is made from three tiny squares (template A), three medium sized

rectangles (template B), one long strip (template C) and one small rectangle (template D). See page 81 for templates.
Row D is made from one small rectangle, one large rectangular appliquéd block, one small square appliquéd block (see page 82 for appliqué templates), one medium rectangle and one pieced block. The pieced block is made from one long strip (template C), one small oblong (template G), two small rectangles (template H), two strips (template I), one very thin strip (template J), one square (template K) and one larger rectangle (template L). See pages 81, 82 and 83 for templates.
Row E is made from one large rectangle, one small rectangle, one very large rectangle and one medium rectangle.

Templates

Row A

A B C D E

square flower block cut
6½ in x 6½ in
(16.5cm x 16.5cm)

stripe direction

large rectangular
flower block cut
6½ in x 16½ in
(16.5cm x 42cm)

small rectangle cut
4½ in x 6½ in
(11.5cm x16.5cm)

Row B

F

large rectangle cut
3½ in x 15 ⅜ in
(9cm x 39cm)

medium rectangle cut
3½ in x 9½ in
(9cm x 24cm)

small rectangle cut
3½ in x 4½ in
(9cm x 1 1.5cm)

CUTTING OUT

Row A:

Template A: cut 12 in SC 08 and 6 in SC 09.

Template B: cut 6 in SC 12 and 12 in SC 20.

Template C: cut 6 in SC 26.

Template D: cut 6 in SC 27.

Template E: cut 6 in SC 14.

Cut 6 square blocks 6½in x 6½in (16.5cm x 16.5cm) in SC 09.

Cut 6 large rectangular blocks 6½in x 16½in (16.5cm x 42cm) BWS 01 (with stripes running along long edges).

Cut 6 small rectangles 4½in x 6½in (11.5cm x 16.5cm) in SC 27.

Cut 6 large flower heads in SC 08 and 6 small in SC 14.

Cut 6 large flower centres in SC 12 and 6 small in SC 07.

Cut 6 long stems in RS 03 (with horizontal stripes).

Cut 6 short stems in SC 21.

Cut 24 large leaves in RS 03 (with horizontal stripes).

Cut 12 small leaves in SC 21.

Row B:

Template F: 4 in SC 08, SC 12, SC 20, SC 26 and SC 27. Cut 8 in SC 14.

Cut 4 large rectangles 3½in x 15⅜in (9cm x 39cm) in SC 07.

Cut 4 medium rectangles 3½in x 9½in (9cm x 24cm) in SC 14.

Cut 4 small rectangles 3½in x 4½in (9cm x 11.5cm) in SC 03.

Row C:

Template A: cut 8 in SC 08 and 4 in SC 09.

Template B: cut 4 in SC 12 and 8 in SC 20.

Template C: cut 4 in SC 26.

Template D: cut 4 in SC 27.

Cut 4 large rectangular blocks 5¼in x 22½in (13.5cm x 57cm) in SC 03.

Cut 4 small rectangular blocks 4½in x 5¼in (11.5cm x 13.5cm) in SC 08.

Cut 4 large flower heads in SC 07.

Cut 4 large flower centres in SC 09.

Cut 4 long stems in RS 03 (with horizontal stripes).

Cut 8 large leaves in RS 03 (with horizontal stripes).

Row D:

Template C: cut 4 in SC 27.

Template I: cut 4 in SC 14 and SC 26.

Template K: cut 4 in SC 08.

Template L: cut 4 in SC 07.

Template J: cut 4 in SC 27.

Template H: cut 8 in SC 12.

Template G: cut 4 in SC 07.

Cut 4 small rectangles 2½in x 6¼in (6.5cm x 16cm) in SC 20.

Cut 4 large rectangles 6¼in x 18¾in (16cm x 47.5cm) in BWS 01 (with stripes running along the long edges).

Cut 4 small squares 6¼in x 6¼in (16cm x 16cm) in SC 09.

Cut 4 medium rectangles 4½in x 6¼in (11.5cm x 16cm) in SC 12.

Cut 4 large flower heads in SC 07 and 4 small in SC 14.

Cut 4 large flower centres in SC 07 and 4 small in SC 14.

Cut 4 long stems in RS 03 (with horizontal stripes).

Cut 4 short stems in SC 21.

Cut 8 large leaves in RS 03 (with horizontal stripes).

Cut 8 small leaves in SC 21.

Row E:

Cut 4 large rectangles 3½in x 14¾in (9cm x 36.5cm) in SC 07.

Cut 4 small rectangles 2½in x 3½in (6.5cm x 9cm) in SC 14.

Cut 4 very large rectangles 3½in x 16½in (9cm x 42cm) in SC 21.

Cut 4 medium rectangles 3½in x 4½in (9cm x 11.5cm) in SC 14.

Borders:

Cut 4 end strips 26in x 4in (66cm x 10cm) and 4 side strips 36½in x 4in (93cm x 10cm) in SC 21.

Corner squares:

Cut 4in x 4in (10cm x 10cm) in SC 08.

Straight cut binding:

Cut 7 strips 2½in- (6.5cm-) wide x width of fabric in NC 03, to form 8¾yds (8m) of binding.

Backing:

Cut 2 pieces 43in x 64in (110cm x 163cm) in NC 03.

Row C

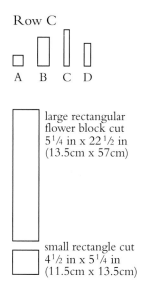

A B C D

large rectangular flower block cut 5¼ in x 22½ in (13.5cm x 57cm)

small rectangle cut 4½ in x 5¼ in (11.5cm x 13.5cm)

Row D

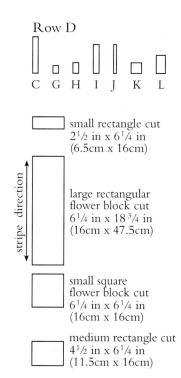

C G H I J K L

small rectangle cut 2½ in x 6¼ in (6.5cm x 16cm)

stripe direction

large rectangular flower block cut 6¼ in x 18¾ in (16cm x 47.5cm)

small square flower block cut 6¼ in x 6¼ in (16cm x 16cm)

medium rectangle cut 4½ in x 6¼ in (11.5cm x 16cm)

Row E

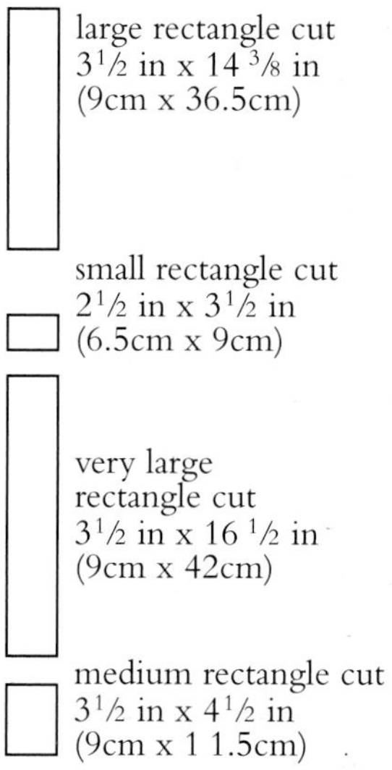

large rectangle cut 3½ in x 14 ⅜ in (9cm x 36.5cm)

small rectangle cut 2½ in x 3½ in (6.5cm x 9cm)

very large rectangle cut 3½ in x 16½ in (9cm x 42cm)

medium rectangle cut 3½ in x 4½ in (9cm x 11.5cm)

Row A
Strip block assembly

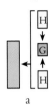

a

b

d

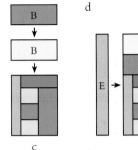

c

Row B
Strip block assembly

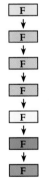

Row C
Strip block assembly

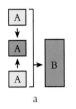
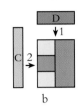

a

b

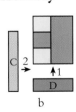

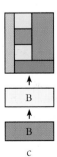

c

Row D
Strip block assembly

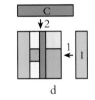

a

b

c

d

MAKING THE STRIP BLOCKS

Using a ¼in (6mm) seam allowance make up 6 row A strip blocks, 4 row B strip blocks, 4 row C strip blocks and 4 row D strip blocks, following the strip block assembly diagrams left.

MAKING THE QUILT ROWS

Using a ¼in (6mm) seam allowance, assemble the plain blocks and strip blocks to form 6 row A's, 4 row B's, 4 row C's, 4 row D's and 4 row E's (see below).

APPLIQUÉ THE ROWS

Hand appliqué (see page 97) rows A, C and D with large and small flowers, using the row assembly diagrams as a placement and fabric guide (see below).

ASSEMBLING THE ROWS

Arrange the rows in two sets of 11 following the quilt assembly diagram. Using a ¼in (6mm) seam allowance, join the rows together and then the two sets of rows to form the quilt centre (right).

Row A assembly	Row B assembly	Row C assembly	Row D assembly	Row E assembly
		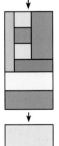	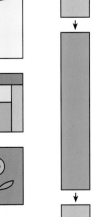	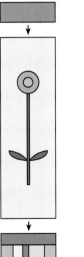

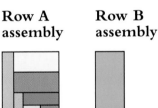
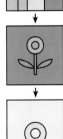
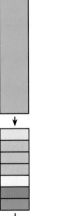

Quilt assembly

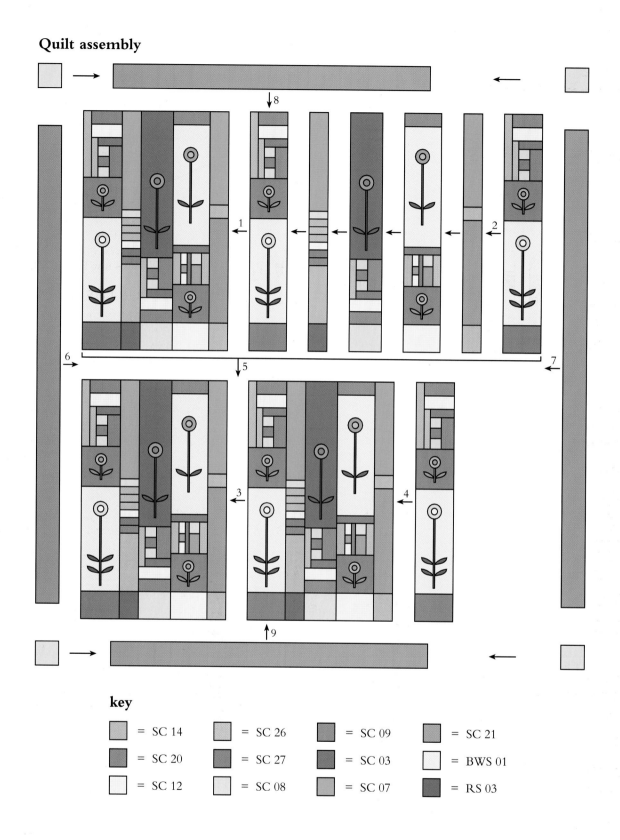

key

= SC 14	= SC 26	= SC 09	= SC 21
= SC 20	= SC 27	= SC 03	= BWS 01
= SC 12	= SC 08	= SC 07	= RS 03

MAKING THE BORDERS

Using a ¼in (6mm) seam allowance, join the end borders to form 2 strips 51½in (131cm) long and the side borders to form two strips 72½in (185cm) long. Attach the two side borders to the edges of the quilt. Join a corner square to each end of the end borders and attach the borders to the ends of the quilt top.

FINISHING THE QUILT

Press the assembled quilt top. Seam the two backing pieces together with a ⅜in (1cm) seam allowance to form one piece approximately 64in x 85in (153cm x 216cm). Layer the quilt top, batting and backing, and baste together (see page 98). Using a toning thread, stitch-in-the-ditch around each row and the edges of the borders (see page 102). Trim the quilt edges and attach the binding (see page 99).

15

Spring Garden

Liza Prior Lucy

★★

This quilt is as fresh and pretty as a spring garden, with its combinations of leafy greens and big florals. The ombre stripes used in this quilt create an effect of a tiled pathway edged with flower borders. The flower blocks themselves are fussy cut from Flower Lattice. Refer to photograph for placement of the individual flowers, but you can 'plant' your garden in any way you choose.

SIZE OF QUILT
The finished quilt will measure approximately 93½in x 93½in (238cm x 238cm).

MATERIALS
Patchwork fabrics:
GP 02-L: ¼yd (23cm) or 1FQ
GP 02-P: ¼yd (23cm) or 1FQ
GP 02-C: ¼yd (23cm) or 1FQ
GP 03-L: ¼yd (23cm) or 1FQ
GP 03-P: ¼yd (23cm) or 1FQ
GP 03-C: ¼yd (23cm) or 1FQ
GP 03-S: ¼yd (23cm) or 1FQ
GP 08-L: ¼yd (23cm) or 1FQ
GP 08-C: ¼yd (23cm) or 1FQ
GP 11-L: 5yds (4.5m)
BWS 01: See binding
OS 01: 1½yds (1.35m) or 6FQ
OS 04: 1½yds (1.35m) or 6FQ
Backing:
GP 06-S: 6½yds (5.85m)
Bias binding:
BWS 01: 1¾yds (1.6m)
Thin batting:
99½in x 99½in (253cm x 253cm)
Quilting thread:
Toning machine quilting thread.

Templates

stripe directions

X   Y   Z

PATCH SHAPES
The quilt centre is made from one small square (template X).
The edges of quilt centre and outer edges of the entire quilt are bordered by large triangles (template Z). The remainder of the quilt is formed by a large square (template Y). See pages 85 and 86 for templates.

CUTTING OUT
Template X: Cut 2⅝in- (6.7cm-) wide strips across width of fabric. Each strip will give you 16 patches per 45in- (114cm-) wide fabric, or 8 per FQ (see page 94).
Cut 18 in GP 02-P and GP 08-L, 22 in GP 03-S, 23 in GP 03-L and GP 08-C, 29 in GP 02-L and GP 02-C, 30 in GP 03-C and 35 in GP 03-P.
Fussy cut (see page 94) 29 in GP 11-L, centralising the flowers.
Template Z: Cut 4⅞in- (12.4cm-) wide strips across width of fabric. Each strip will give you 7 patches per 45in- (114cm-) wide fabric, or 3 per FQ.
Cut 60 in BWS 01.
Template Y: Cut 6½in- (16.5cm-) wide strips across width of fabric. Each strip will give you 6 patches per 45in- (114cm-) wide fabric, or 3 per FQ.
Cut 48 in OS 01 and OS 04.
Fussy cut (see page 94) 84 in GP 11-L, centralising the flowers.
Backing:
Cut 2 pieces 45in x 99½in (114cm x 253cm) and 3 pieces 33½in x 12in (86cm x 30.5cm) in GP 06-S.
Bias binding:
Cut 10½yds (9.6m) of bias binding 2¼in- (6cm-) wide from BWS 01.

MAKING THE QUILT CENTRE
Arrange 16 small square patches (template X) in 16 rows following the quilt assembly guide. Using a ¼in (6mm) seam allowance join the patches into 16 rows, then join the rows together to form the quilt centre.

COMPLETING THE QUILT TOP
To form the 4 triangular sections that fit the sides of the quilt centre, arrange 6 large squares (template Y) in 3 diagonal rows, edged with 4 large triangles (template Z) - see the quilt assembly diagram, right. **Important**: make sure stripes lie in the right direction. Using a ¼in (6mm) seam allowance, assemble the rows and attach to quilt centre.
Using the quilt assembly diagram as a guide, make up the 4 large corner sections of the quilt, by arranging 6 rows of large squares (template Y) with a large triangle (template Z) at each end of the rows. **Important**: make sure stripes lie in the right direction. Join rows together and seam the remaining large triangles together in 2's to form each corner. Join made up sections to quilt top in the order shown on the quilt assembly diagram.

FINISHING THE QUILT
Press the assembled quilt top. Seam the 5 backing pieces of fabric together with a ⅜in (1cm) seam allowance to form one piece approximately 99½in x 99½in (253cm x 253cm).
Layer the quilt top, batting and backing, and baste together (see page 98).
Stitch-in-the-ditch around the quilt

Quilt assembly

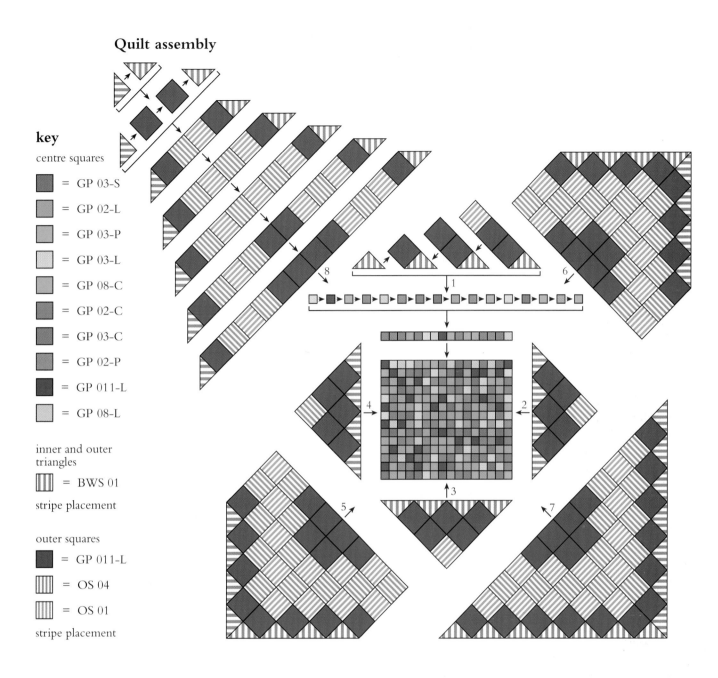

key

centre squares

■	=	GP 03-S
■	=	GP 02-L
■	=	GP 03-P
■	=	GP 03-L
■	=	GP 08-C
■	=	GP 02-C
■	=	GP 03-C
■	=	GP 02-P
■	=	GP 011-L
■	=	GP 08-L

inner and outer triangles

▥	=	BWS 01

stripe placement

outer squares

■	=	GP 011-L
▥	=	OS 04
▥	=	OS 01

stripe placement

Quilting inner triangles

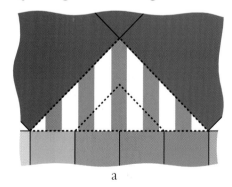

a

Quilting outer triangles

b

Quilting large squares

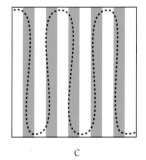

c

centre, then free-motion quilt over the quilt centre in a very random fashion working across 2 rows of the small squares at a time.

Stitch-in-ditch around inner triangles and

work another triangular row approximately 1½in (4cm) in - see quilting diagram (a). Loosely stitch around each flower shape on the large floral squares and free-motion quilt the

remaining large squares and outer triangles, following the stripe directions - see quilting diagrams (b) and (c).

Trim the quilt edges and attach the binding (see page 99).

17

Spring Garden
by Liza Prior Lucy
Instructions on page 16

Chequer-board Bag

KAFFE FASSETT

Kaffe decided he wanted to create a simple all-purpose bag that would go with lots of different outfits. The result is this stylish project made from the shot cotton fabrics in soft driftwood tones. It is a very easy bag to construct, using just one simple square and lined with a lovely two-tone Rowan shot cotton. To finish off Kaffe hand-quilted the sides in a naive spiral fashion.

SIZE OF BAG
The finished bag will measure approximately 12in x 15in (30.5cm x 38cm).

MATERIALS
Patchwork fabrics:
SC 23: ½yd (45cm) or 2FQ
SC 29: ⅛yd (15cm) or 1FQ
SC 31: ⅛yd (15cm) or 1FQ
SC 33: ⅛yd (15cm) or 1FQ
SC 36: ⅛yd (15cm) or 1FQ
RS 01: ⅛yd (15cm) or 1FQ
RS 04: See lining
ES 04: ⅛yd (15cm) or 1FQ
Lining:
RS 04: ⅔yd (60cm) or 2FQ
Batting:
½yd (45cm) x 45in (114cm) wide
Quilting thread:
Stranded embroidery thread in terracotta.

Template

Q

PATCH SHAPES
The bag is made of 1 square patch shape (template Q). See page 83 for template.

CUTTING OUT
Template Q: Cut 4 in SC 29, SC 31 and ES 04. Cut 5 in RS 01, RS 04 and SC 33. Cut 6 in SC 36. Cut 33 in SC 23.

Lining:
For the front and back bag, cut 2 pieces 12½in x 15½in (32cm x 39.5cm) in RS 04. For the gussets, cut 2 side pieces 3½in x 15½in (9cm x 39.5cm) and 1 base piece 3½in x 12½in (9cm x 32cm) in RS 04. For the strap, cut 2 pieces 3½in x 18½in (9cm x 47cm) in RS 04.

Batting:
For the front and back bag, cut 2 pieces 12½in x 15½in (32cm x 39.5cm). For the gussets, cut 2 side pieces 3½in x 15½in (9cm x 39.5cm) and 1 base piece 3½in x 12½in (9cm x 32cm). For the strap cut 1 piece 3½in x 36½in (9cm x 93cm).

Bag assembly

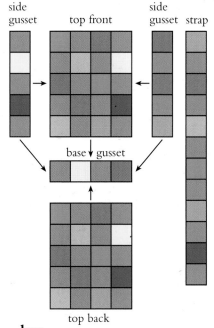

side gusset   top front   side gusset   strap

base gusset

top back

key
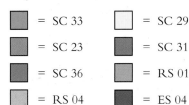

= SC 33   = SC 29

= SC 23   = SC 31

= SC 36   = RS 01

= RS 04   = ES 04

ASSEMBLING BAG PIECES
Using a ¼in (6mm) seam allowance assemble 4 rows of 5 patches and join rows to form the front bag, using bag assembly diagrams as a guide. Repeat for back bag. Assemble 2 rows of 5 patches for the side gussets, 1 row of 4 patches for the base and 1 row of 12 patches for the strap, using the bag assembly diagram as a guide.

QUILTING THE BAG
Press the assembled patchwork tops. Layer the front, back and gusset tops with the batting, and baste together (see page 98). Using 3 strands of the embroidery thread work a hand quilted spiral row of stitches on the front and back bags, starting at the centre and spacing spirals ½in apart out to the centre (see quilting diagram below). For the gussets, work 4 hand quilted rows along length, evenly spaced

FINISHING OFF THE BAG
For full instructions on how to complete the bag, turn to page 100. Quilt straps to match gussets.

Quilting

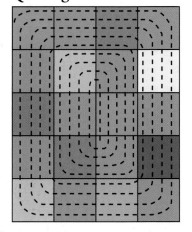

Chequer-board Bag
by Kaffe Fassett

Nine Patch Stripe
by Pauline Smith

Nine Patch Stripe

PAULINE SMITH

This quilt is based on the traditional nine-patch Amish quilt design. It is very easy to make – just play around with the colours to form your own combinations, adding a rogue colour for impact. For speed you can sew your rotary-cut strips together in rows of 3 and cut through at 2⅛in (5.5cm) intervals to form rows of 2⅛in (5.5cm) squares.

SIZE OF QUILT

The finished quilt will measure approximately 84in x 93in (213cm x 236cm).

MATERIALS

Patchwork fabrics:
SC 01: ⅛yd (15cm) or 1FQ
SC 05: ½yd (45cm) or 2FQ
SC 08: ¼yd (23cm) or 1FQ
SC 11: ⅛yd (15cm) or 1FQ
SC 14: ⅛yd (15cm) or 1FQ
SC 20: see outer borders
SC 23: ⅛yd (15cm) or 1FQ
SC 24: See inner borders
SC 26: See inner borders
SC 27: ¼yd (23cm) or 1FQ
SC 29: See inner borders
SC 36: ⅓yd (30cm) or 1FQ
RS 01: ⅓yd (30cm) or 2FQ
RS 04: See backing fabric
RS 06: ⅓yd (30cm) or 2FQ
Inner borders:
SC 24: 1⅛yds (1.05m)
SC 26: 1yd (90cm)
SC 29: 1⅛yds (1.05m)
Outer borders:
SC 20: 1¾yds (1.6m)
Backing:
RS 04: 6⅔yds (6.00m)
Bias binding:
RS 04: see backing
Batting:
90in x 99in (229cm x 252cm)
Quilting thread:
Toning machine quilting thread.

PATCH SHAPES

The quilt centre is made up of a nine patch pieced block (template A), stitched together in rows with rectangular blocks

Templates

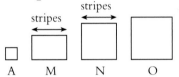

A   M   N   O

(template M) and square blocks (template N). The rows are joined together alternately with straight inner borders. The edges of the quilt are bordered with a square shape at each corner (template O). See pages 81, 84 and 85 for templates.

CUTTING OUT

Template A: Cut 2⅛in- (5.5cm-) wide strips across width of fabric. Each strip will give you 20 patches per 45in- (114cm-) wide fabric, or 10 per FQ (see page 94).
Cut 15 in SC 23, 19 in SC 14, 20 in SC 11, 23 in SC 01, 39 in SC 08, 44 in SC 27, 65 in SC 26, 77 in SC 24, 78 in SC 29, 80 in SC 36, 82 in SC 20 and 106 in SC 05.
Template M: Cut 16 in RS 01 and RS 06. Cut 32 in RS 04.
Template N: Cut 4 in RS 01 and RS 06. Cut 8 in RS 04.
Template O: Cut 4 in SC 29.
Inner borders:
Cut 4 inner border strips 5¼in x 40⅝in (13.5cm x 106cm) in SC 26 and SC 29. Cut 6 inner border strips in SC 24.
Outer borders:
Cut 4 side border strips 7in x 40⅝in (18cm x 106cm) in SC 20. Cut 4 end border strips 7in x 36in (18cm x 91.5cm) in SC 20.
Backing:
Cut 2 pieces 45in x 99in (114cm x 252cm) in RS 04.

Bias binding:

Cut 10yds (9m) of bias binding 2½in- (6.5cm-) wide from RS 04.

MAKING THE NINE PATCH BLOCKS

Using a ¼in (6mm) seam allowance, make up 72 blocks, using the block and quilt assembly diagrams as a guide.

MAKING THE QUILT ROWS

Using a ¼in (6mm) seam allowance, assemble 8 rows of 9 nine patch blocks alternating with 8 rectangular blocks (template M) and a square block (template N) at each end. Use the quilt assembly diagram as a guide.
Using a ¼in (6mm) seam allowance, join the inner borders to form 7 strips 80¾in (205cm) long.

Block assembly

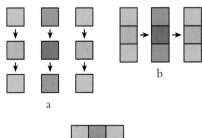

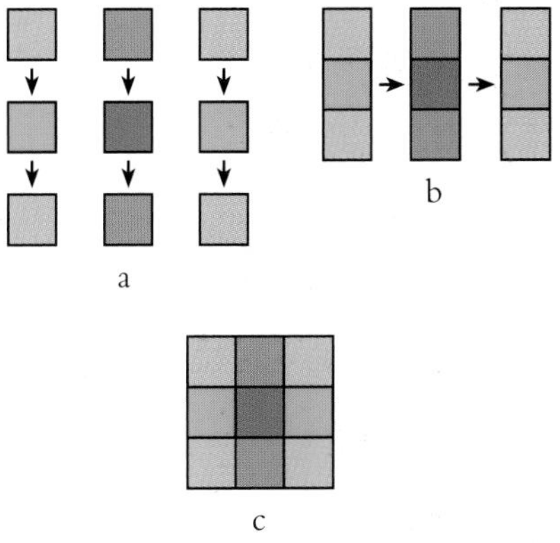

a   b

c

ASSEMBLING THE ROWS

Arrange the pieced rows alternately with the inner borders following the quilt assembly diagram. Using a ¼in (6mm) seam allowance, join the rows and borders together to form the quilt centre.

MAKING THE OUTER BORDERS

Using a ¼in (6mm) seam allowance, join the end borders to form 2 strips 71½in (182cm) long and the side borders to form 2 strips 80¾in (205cm) long. Attach the 2 end borders to the edges of the quilt. Join a corner square (template O) to each end of the side borders and attach to the sides of the quilt top.

FINISHING THE QUILT

Press the assembled quilt top. Seam the 2 backing pieces together with a ⅜in (1cm) seam allowance to form one piece approximately 89in x 99in (227cm x 252cm).

Layer the quilt top, batting and backing, and baste together (see page 98). Using a toning thread, stitch-in-the-ditch down each row and around the edges of the borders (see page 102).

Trim the quilt edges and attach the binding (see page 99).

Quilt assembly

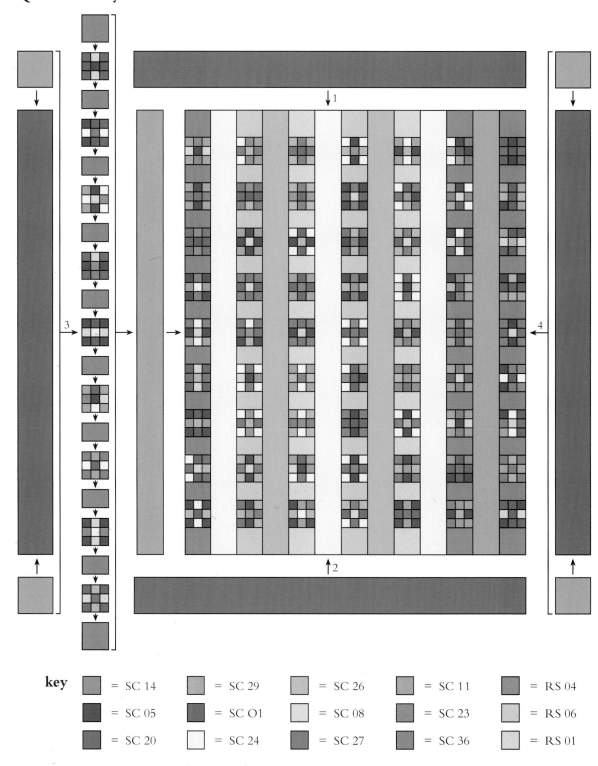

key				
= SC 14	= SC 29	= SC 26	= SC 11	= RS 04
= SC 05	= SC O1	= SC 08	= SC 23	= RS 06
= SC 20	= SC 24	= SC 27	= SC 36	= RS 01

Pin Wheel Star
by Kaffe Fassett
Instructions on page 26

Pin Wheel Star

KAFFE FASSETT

The pin wheel star is a design from an old classic quilt. It is usually worked in just two colours, with the triangles in each unit placed alternately to create a windmill shape. Kaffe has used two main plain colours for this quilt, but has chosen various soft prints to work with them in the small units. This quilt is very easy to make - the trick is in the placing of the units to form the star shapes.

SIZE OF QUILT
The finished quilt will measure approximately 73in x 90in (185.5cm x 201.5cm).

MATERIALS
Patchwork fabrics:
GP 01-P: ¼yd (23cm) or 1FQ
GP 01-G: ¼yd (23cm) or 1FQ
GP 01-PK: ¼yd (23cm) or 1FQ
GP 02-C: ¼yd (23cm) or 1FQ
GP 02-P: see backing
GP 04-P: ¼yd (23cm) or 1FQ
GP 06-P: ¼yd (23cm) or 1FQ
GP 06-J: ¼yd (23cm) or 1FQ
GP 06-S: ¼yd (23cm) or 1FQ
GP 07-P: ¼yd (23cm) or 1FQ
GP 08-C: ½yd (46cm) or 2FQ
GP 08-L: ¼yd (23cm) or 1FQ
SC 17: 3½yds (3.2m) or 16FQ
SC 36: 2yds (1.8m) or 8FQ

Backing:
GP 02-P: 5½yds (5m)

Bias binding:
RS 05: ⅓yd (30cm)

Batting:
80in x 96in (203cm x 244cm)

Quilting thread:
Toning machine quilting thread

Templates

KK   LL

PATCH SHAPES
The quilt top is made from 2 sizes of pin wheel units. The small pin wheels are made from 1 small triangle (template KK)

and the large from a large triangle (template LL). See page 88 for templates.

CUTTING OUT
Template KK: Cut 3in- (7.5cm-) wide strips across width of fabric. Each strip will give you 30 patches per 45in- (114cm-) wide fabric, or 14 per FQ (see page 94).
Cut 80 in SC 36, 40 in GP 01-G, 41 in GP 06-J, 42 in GP 06-S, 43 in GP 08-L, 48 in GP 01-PK and GP 04-P, 50 in GP 01-P, 53 in GP 07-P and GP 06-P, 54 in GP 02-C, 59 in GP 02-P and 97 in GP 08-C. Cut 708 in SC 17.
Template LL: Cut 7¼in- (18.5cm-) wide strips across width of fabric. Each strip will give you 12 patches per 45in- (114cm-) wide fabric, or 6 per FQ (see page 94).
Cut 80 in SC 17 and SC 36.

Backing:
Cut 2 pieces 45in x 96in (114cm x 244cm) in GP 02-P.

Bias binding:
Cut 9⅛yds (8.25m) of bias binding 2½- (6.5cm-) wide from RS 05.

MAKING THE PIN WHEEL UNITS
Using a ¼in (6mm) seam allowance make up 18 small pin wheel units with 4 patches of SC 17, 1 patch of SC 36 and 3 patches of another colour; make up 31 small units with 4 patches of SC 17, 2 patches of SC 36 and 2 patches of another colour and finally 128 small units with 4 patches of SC 17 and 4 patches of another colour. Use quilt assembly diagram as a colour guide (see right).

Large and small pin wheel unit assembly

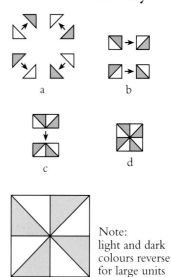

Note:
light and dark
colours reverse
for large units

In the same way make up 20 large pin wheel units following the unit assembly diagrams, making sure you have reversed the positions of the SC 17 patches from the small pin wheel units.

MAKING THE PIN WHEEL BLOCKS
Using a ¼in (6mm) seam allowance, assemble 12 pin wheel blocks, using the block assembly and quilt assembly diagrams as a guide (see right). Make sure all these blocks contain two small pin wheel units with 2 coloured patches.
NOTE: it is very important to position the SC 36 patches as shown in diagrams. Assemble 3 blocks in the same way, with one small pin wheel unit having 2 colours along the base and one unit having

3 colours along the left hand side.
Assemble 4 blocks with one small pin wheel unit having 2 colours along the left hand side and one unit having 3 colours along the base.
Assemble 1 block with 2 small pin wheel units having 3 colours.
Finally assemble 9 rows of 4 small pin wheel units, each containing 1 small unit with 3 coloured patches. You should be left with just 1 small unit for the corner.

Block assembly

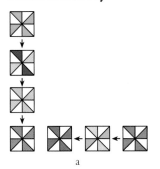
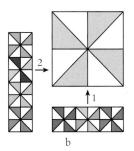
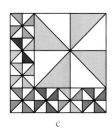

a   b   c

Quilt assembly

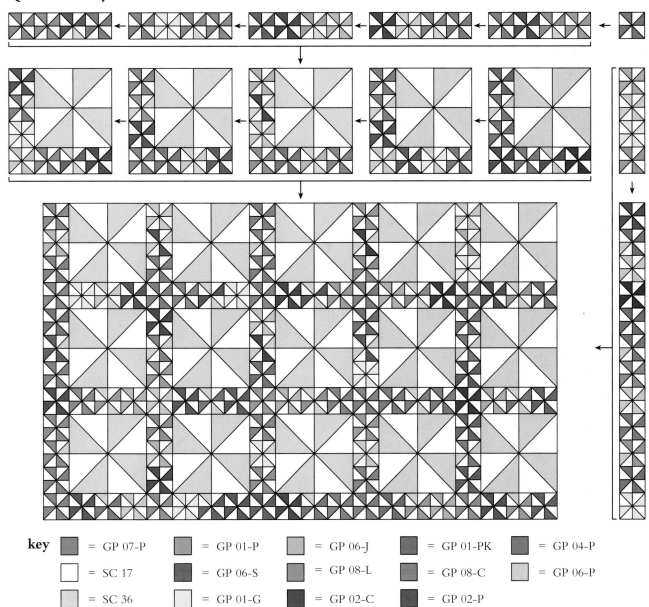

key

■ = GP 07-P	■ = GP 01-P	■ = GP 06-J	■ = GP 01-PK	■ = GP 04-P
□ = SC 17	■ = GP 06-S	■ = GP 08-L	■ = GP 08-C	■ = GP 06-P
■ = SC 36	□ = GP 01-G	■ = GP 02-C	■ = GP 02-P	

ASSEMBLING THE BLOCKS

Using quilt assembly diagram as a guide, arrange 4 rows of 5 blocks, making sure you have blocks positioned in the right places. Using a ¼in (6mm) seam allowance, join blocks into 4 rows. Then, join rows together to form the main part of quilt. To form top and right hand borders, arrange 5 sets of small blocks in one row and 4 sets in another row. Join sets together to form 2 rows. Stitch shorter row to right hand edge of quilt. Add remaining small pin wheel unit to right hand end of the longer row and join this to top edge of the quilt.

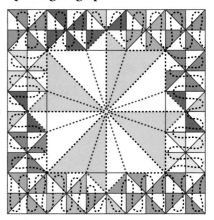

FINISHING THE QUILT

Press the assembled quilt top. Seam the 2 backing pieces together with a ⅜in (1cm) seam allowance to form one piece approximately 80in x 96in (203cm x 244cm). Layer the quilt top, batting and backing, and baste together (see page 98). Using a toning thread, stitch-in-the-ditch around each patch of all large pin wheel units, diagonally across each patch to enable you to stitch-in-the-ditch around each SC 17 and SC 36 patches in the adjacent small pin wheel units, creating a kite-like effect. This should be easy to do if you have assembled the blocks correctly (see quilting diagram). Free-motion quilt in a squiggle fashion around the remaining borders of small units (see quilting diagram). Trim the quilt edges and attach the binding (see page 99).

Sail Away

KAFFE FASSETT

★★

The new Rowan stripe fabrics reminded Kaffe of flags, and flags made him think of sails in a lovely soft, faded palette. So the idea of a sail boat bordered with flag shapes was born. The central picture square is formed simply by a combination of both patchwork and appliqué, and the rest of the quilt from one basic triangle. This project would look good in a child's room, or a bathroom.

SIZE OF QUILT

The finished quilt will measure approximately 57½in x 57½in (146cm x 146cm).

MATERIALS

Patchwork and appliqué fabrics:
SC 14: ⅛yd (15cm) or 1FQ
SC 24: ⅔yd (60cm) or 3FQ
SC 28: ⅔yd (60cm) or 3FQ
SC 33: ⅛yd (15cm) or 1FQ
SC 35: ¼yd (23cm) or 1FQ
OS 01: ¼yd (23cm) or 1FQ
OS 02: ¼yd (23cm) or 1FQ
OS 04: ¼yd (23cm) or 1FQ
OS 05: ¼yd (23cm) or 1FQ

BWS 01: ⅔yd (60cm) or 3FQ
BWS 02: See backing
RS 01: ¼yd (23cm) or 1FQ
RS 02: ¼yd (23cm) or 1FQ
RS 04: ¼yd (23cm) or 1FQ
RS 05: ¼yd (23cm) or 1FQ
RS 06: ¼yd (23cm) or 1FQ
RS 07: ¼yd (23cm) or 1FQ
RS 08: ¼yd (23cm) or 1FQ
Backing:
BWS 02: 3yds (2.7m)
Straight cut binding:
PR 02: ½yd (45cm)
Batting:
63in x 63in (160cm x 160cm)
Quilting thread:
Toning machine quilting thread

Templates

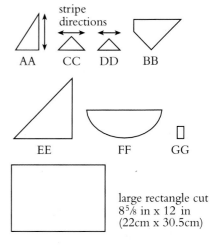

stripe directions

AA   CC   DD   BB

EE   FF   GG

large rectangle cut
8⅝ in x 12 in
(22cm x 30.5cm)

Sail Away
by Kaffe Fassett

PATCH SHAPES

The central picture block is formed by a mixture of patchwork and appliqué. The sea is formed by 4 tiny triangles (template DD) and 2 small triangles (template CC). The boat is 2 'chopped-off' triangles (template BB); the sky, 2 small triangles (template CC) and a large rectangle. The sun is formed by a semi-circle (template FF); the mast a tiny strip (template GG); and the sail a large triangle (template EE). The remainder of the quilt and border is made from 1 right-angled triangle (template AA). See pages 86 and 87 for templates.

CUTTING OUT

Template AA: Cut 7⅛in- (18cm-) wide strips across width of fabric. Each strip will give you 24 patches per 45in- (114cm-) wide fabric, or 12 per FQ (see page 94).
Cut 7 in OS 01 and OS 04, 11 in RS 01, 13 in RS 06, 17 in RS 04, 19 in OS 05 and RS 05, 20 in OS 02 and RS 07, 21 in RS 08, 22 in RS 02, 24 in BWS 02, 60 in SC 24 and SC28, and 64 in BWS 01.
Template BB: Cut 1 template in SC 14, and 1 template reversed in SC 14.
Template CC: Cut 2 in BWS 02 and SC 35.
Template DD: Cut 4 in BWS 02.
Template EE: Cut 1 in SC 28.
Template FF: Cut 1 in SC 33.
Template GG: Cut 1 from a brown stripe on OS 01.
Centre square sky:
Cut 1 large rectangle 8⅝in x 12in (22cm x 30.5cm) in SC 35.
Backing:
Cut 1 piece 45in x 63in (114cm x 160cm) and 2 pieces 20in x 32in (51cm x 81cm) in BWS 02.
Straight cut binding:
Cut 6 strips 2½in- (6.5cm-) wide x width of fabric in PR 02, to form 6½yds (5.85m) of binding.

MAKING THE CENTRAL PICTURE BLOCK

Using a ¼in (6mm) seam allowance, make up the patchwork section following steps a, b, c, and d of the central picture block assembly diagrams. Then, machine appliqué (see page 97) the mast, sun and sail in place following steps e and f of the central picture block assembly diagrams.

Centre picture block assembly

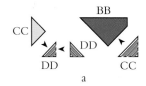

a

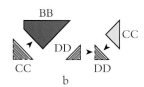

b

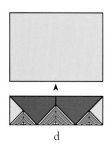

c

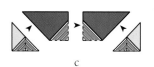

d

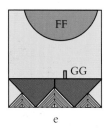

e

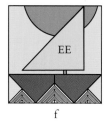

f

MAKING THE TRIANGLE BLOCKS

Using a ¼in (6mm) seam allowance, assemble 60 central triangular blocks by joining 4 right-angled triangles, as shown in the triangle block assembly diagram, and using the quilt assembly diagram as a fabric guide. Assemble 32 border blocks and 4 corner blocks in the same way.

Triangle block assembly

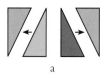

a

b   c

ASSEMBLING THE CENTRE BLOCKS

Using quilt assembly diagram as a guide, arrange 6 central triangular blocks into 2 rows of 3. Using a ¼in (6mm) seam allowance, join blocks into rows and then join rows together. Stitch to top of central picture block. Repeat with 6 more blocks and attach to base of central picture block. Following the quilt assembly diagram as a guide, arrange 6 rows of 8 central triangular blocks. Using a ¼in (6mm) seam allowance, join the blocks into the 6 rows. Join rows together in 2 sets of 3 and attach to each side of quilt to form quilt centre.

ASSEMBLING THE BORDER BLOCKS

Arrange the triangular border blocks into 4 rows of 8 blocks, following the quilt assembly diagram. Using a ¼in (6mm) seam allowance, join the blocks to form 4 border strips. Attach 2 borders to the sides of the quilt. Stitch a stripey corner block to each end of the remaining 2 border strips and attach to the top and base of quilt.

FINISHING THE QUILT

Press the assembled quilt top. Seam 3 backing pieces together with a ³⁄₈in (1cm) seam allowance to form one piece approximately 63in x 63in (160cm x 160cm).

Layer the quilt top, batting and backing, and baste together (see page 98).
Using a toning thread, stitch-in-the-ditch around the edges of each SC 24, SC 28, and BWS 01 right-angled patches (see

page 102). Stitch-in-the-ditch around the inner edge of the border and outer edge of the central picture square.
Trim the quilt edges and attach the binding (see page 99).

Quilt assembly

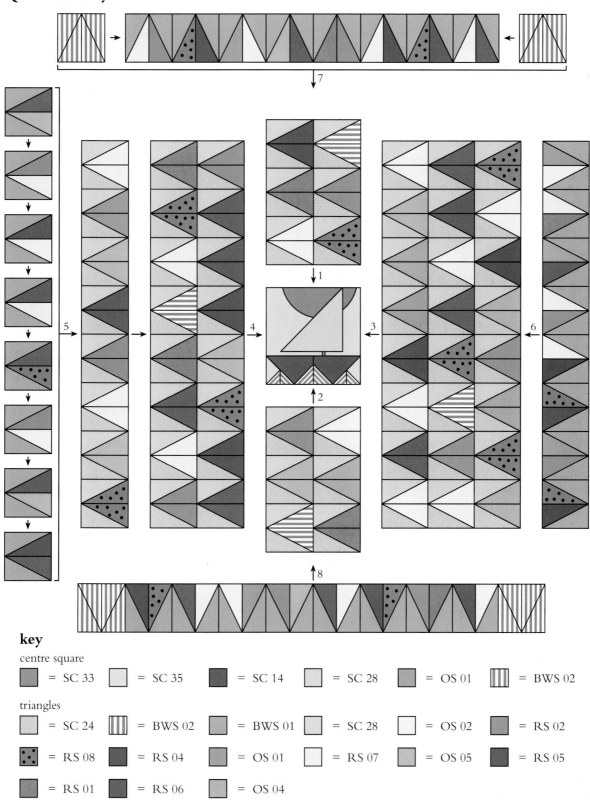

key

centre square

■ = SC 33 □ = SC 35 ■ = SC 14 □ = SC 28 ■ = OS 01 ▥ = BWS 02

triangles

□ = SC 24 ▥ = BWS 02 ■ = BWS 01 □ = SC 28 □ = OS 02 ■ = RS 02

⁘ = RS 08 ■ = RS 04 ■ = OS 01 □ = RS 07 ■ = OS 05 ■ = RS 05

■ = RS 01 ■ = RS 06 □ = OS 04

TRADITIONAL TREASURES

Seven projects in rich autumnal colours, inspired by an old
English lifestyle – think of grand Shakespearean houses, worn
leather, aged oak and faded opulent fabrics

Kaleidoscope
by Kaffe Fassett
Instructions on page 34

Kaleidoscope

KAFFE FASSETT

Kaffe has always loved huge star designs, particularly when the colours blend together lavishly, just like in a childrens' kaleidoscope. The main star section in this quilt is formed by rows of brightly-coloured small diamonds that seem to 'melt together', just as Kaffe wanted. To add extra sparkle to the quilt, he decided to boldly hand-quilt in a contrasting turquoise cotton.

SIZE OF QUILT
The finished quilt will measure approx 97½in x 97½in (248cm x 248cm).

MATERIALS
Patchwork fabrics:
GP 01-G: ¼yd (23cm) or 1FQ
GP 01-BW: ½yd (45cm) or 2FQ
GP 01-R: ¼yd (23cm) or 1FQ
GP 02-J: ⅔yd (60cm) or 2FQ
GP 03-S: ⅓yd (30cm) or 2FQ
GP 04-J: ⅓yd (30cm) or 2FQ
GP 06-J: ⅛yd (15cm) or 1FQ
GP 07-P: ½yd (45cm) or 2FQ
GP 08-J: ⅔yd (60cm) or 2FQ
SC 08: ½yd (45cm) or 2FQ
SC 10: ⅔yd (60cm) or 3FQ
SC 12: ¼yd (23cm) or 1FQ
SC 14: ½yd (45cm) or 2FQ
SC 27: ¼yd (23cm) or 1FQ
SC 33: ½yd (45cm) or 2FQ
RS 02: ⅛yd (15cm) or 1FQ
RS 05: ½yd (45cm) or 2FQ
RS 06: ⅔yd (60cm) or 2FQ
Outer squares and triangles:
SC 16: 5yds (4.5m)
Backing:
PS 13: 7⅓yds (6.6m)
Bias binding:
PS 13: see backing
Batting:
104in x 104in (265cm x 265cm)
Quilting thread:
Turquoise Linen drape, by Rowan

PATCH SHAPES
The central star shape is made from one small diamond (template JJ). See page 88 for template. The outer sections of the star are in-filled with large plain squares and triangles.

Templates

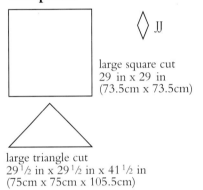

large square cut
29 in x 29 in
(73.5cm x 73.5cm)

large triangle cut
29½ in x 29½ in x 41½ in
(75cm x 75cm x 105.5cm)

CUTTING OUT
Template JJ: Cut 2½in- (6.5cm-) wide strips across width of fabric. Each strip will give you 11 patches per 45in- (114cm-) wide fabric, or 5 per FQ (see Rotary cutting page 94).
Cut 8 patches in GP 06-J and RS 02, 16 in GP 01-G and SC 27, 24 in GP 01-R and SC 12, 32 in GP 04-J, 40 in GP 03-S, 48 in GP 01-BW and SC 33, 56 in GP 07-P and SC 14, 64 in SC 08 and RS 05, 72 in GP 02-J, GP 08-J and RS 06, and 80 in SC 10.
Outer squares:
Cut 4 large squares 29in x 29in (73.5cm x 73.5cm) in SC 16.
Outer triangles:
Cut 4 triangles in 29½in x 29½in x 41½in (75cm x 75cm x 105.5cm) in SC 16.
Backing:
Cut 2 pieces 45in x 104in (114cm x 264cm) and 2 pieces 16in x 52½in (40.5cm x 133.5cm) in PS 13.
Bias binding:
Cut 11yds (9.9m) of bias binding 2½ in- (6cm-) wide from PS 13.

MAKING THE LARGE DIAMOND SECTIONS
Following the key and quilt assembly in strict order, arrange 10 patches in 10 rows. Using a ¼in (6mm) seam, join the patches together into rows, then join the rows together to form one large diamond section. Repeat 8 times until you have made all the diamond sections.

ASSEMBLING THE QUILT
Following the quilt assembly diagram, join the large diamond sections together in 2's (see number 1 on diagram). Using the inset seam method (see page 96), attach a large square into each of the 'V' shapes formed by the 2 diamonds (see number 2 on the diagram). Next, join the sets of diamonds together into 2 sets of 4, then join the 2 sets to form a large star. Finally, using the inset seam method, attach the large triangular sections.

FINISHING THE QUILT
Press the assembled quilt top. Seam the 4 backing fabric pieces together with a ⅜in (1cm) seam allowance to form one piece approximately 104in x 104in (265cm x 265cm).
Layer the quilt top, batting and backing, and baste together (see page 98).
Using 3 or 4 strands of the linen drape thread, and starting at the centre, work horizontal rows of hand quilting stitches across each small diamond patch, creating concentric octagonal rows around the centre of the main star.
Continue working in the same manner across small diamond patches to form parallel rows out to the star points.
On large square corners work

Quilt assembly

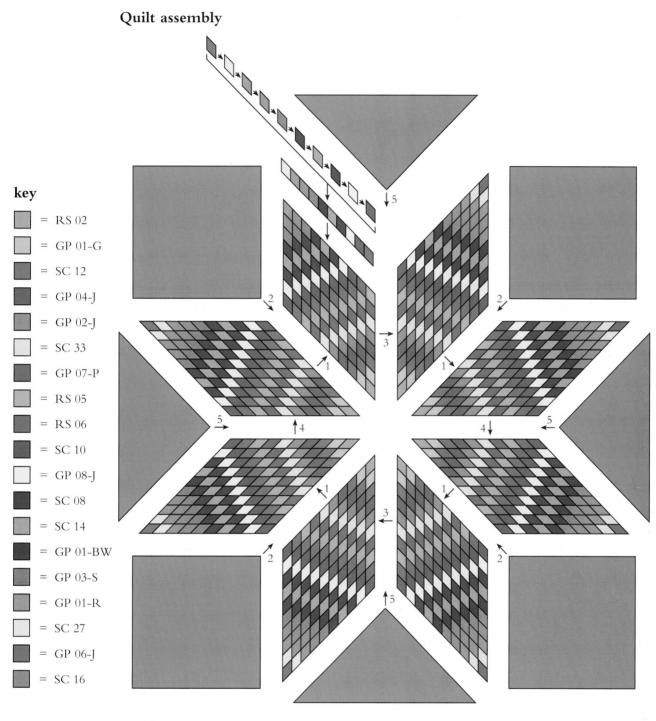

key

■ =	RS 02
■ =	GP 01-G
■ =	SC 12
■ =	GP 04-J
■ =	GP 02-J
■ =	SC 33
■ =	GP 07-P
■ =	RS 05
■ =	RS 06
■ =	SC 10
■ =	GP 08-J
■ =	SC 08
■ =	SC 14
■ =	GP 01-BW
■ =	GP 03-S
■ =	GP 01-R
■ =	SC 27
■ =	GP 06-J
■ =	SC 16

Quilting large squares

inner
corner

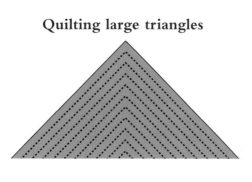

outer
corner

Quilting large triangles

approximately 20 rows of 'L' shaped hand quilting stitches 1½in (4cm) apart, parallel to the outer edges of the quilt. For the large triangles work 11 rows of 'L' shaped stitching, 1½in (4cm) apart, parallel to the inner edges of the triangles (see quilting diagrams).

Trim the quilt edges and attach the binding (see page 99).

Storm At Sea

KAFFE FASSETT

Kaffe originally saw this traditional design, made from dark fabrics on a white background, when he was in Denmark. The design is something of an optical illusion, which gives the appearance of curved seams even though everything is cut straight. Although all the units and blocks are simple to form, it is extremely important to assemble the quilt in strict order so the waves form correctly.

SIZE OF QUILT

The finished quilt will measure approximately 56in x 80in (142cm x 203cm).

MATERIALS

Patchwork fabrics:
GP 01-R: ⅓yd (30cm) or 2FQ
GP 02-J: ¾yd (70cm) or 3FQ
GP 03-L: ⅓yd (30cm) or 2FQ
GP 04-L: ⅓yd (30cm) or 2FQ
GP 04-S: ½yd (45cm) or 3FQ
GP 08-J: ⅓yd (30cm) or 2FQ
GP 09-L: ⅓yd (30cm) or 2FQ
GP 11-C: ½yd (45cm) or 3FQ
PR 04: ⅔yd (60cm) or 3FQ
SC 07: ¾yd (30cm) or 3FQ
SC 16: 1yd (90cm) or 3FQ
SC 27: ¾yd (30cm) or 3FQ
Backing:
NS 01: 4yds (3.6m)
Straight cut binding:
NS 01: see backing
Batting:
62in x 86in (157cm x 218cm)
Quilting thread:
Toning machine quilting thread

Templates

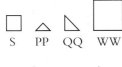

PATCH SHAPES

The quilt top is made from 2 different rows A and B. Each row is made from a different block. Row A blocks are made from 2 units. The first is a larger square unit formed from 1 medium square (template WW), 4 medium sized triangles (template RR) and 4 larger triangles (template SS). The second unit is a diamond unit, formed from a large diamond (template NN) and 4 small right-angled triangles (template OO).
Row B blocks are also made from 2 units. The same diamond unit as used in row A, but turned through 90 degrees, and a smaller square unit. This is formed from 1 small square (template S), 4 tiny triangles (template PP), and 4 small triangles (template QQ).
See pages 82, 89 and 90 for templates.

CUTTING OUT

Template WW: Cut 4⅜in- (11.3cm-) wide strips across width of fabric. Each strip will give you 10 patches per 45in- (114cm-) wide fabric, or 5 per FQ (see page 94). Cut 35 in PR 04.
Template SS: Cut 4⅞in- (12.5cm-) wide strips across width of fabric. Each strip will give you 18 patches per 45in- (114cm-) wide fabric, or 8 per FQ (see page 94).
Cut 22 in GP 02-J, 23 in GP 03-L and GP 04-L, 24 in GP 01-R, GP 08-J and GP 09-L.
Template RR: Cut 3⅝in- (9.2cm-) wide strips across width of fabric. Each strip will give you 24 patches per 45in- (114cm-) wide fabric, or 12 per FQ (see page 94). Cut 140 in SC 16.
Template NN: Cut 4⅛in- (10.5cm-)

wide strips across width of fabric. Each strip will give you 5 patches per 45in- (114cm-) wide fabric, or 2 per FQ (see page 94). Cut 19 in GP 04-S and GP 11-C, and 20 in GP 02-J.
Template OO: Cut 5¼in- (13.3cm-) wide strips across width of fabric. Each strip will give you 32 patches per 45in- (114cm-) wide fabric, or 16 per FQ (see page 94). Cut 56 in SC 27 and 60 in SC 07. With template reversed, cut 56 in SC 07 and 60 in SC 27.
Template S: Cut 2½in- (6.5cm-) wide strips across width of fabric. Each strip will give you 18 patches per 45in- (114cm-) wide fabric, or 9 per FQ (see page 94). Cut 24 in PR 04.
Template PP: Cut 2¼in- (5.8cm-) wide strips across width of fabric. Each strip will give you 40 patches per 45in- (114cm-) wide fabric, or 18 per FQ (see page 94). Cut 96 in SC 16.
Template QQ: Cut 2¾in- (7cm-) wide strips across width of fabric. Each strip will give you 32 patches per 45in- (114cm-) wide fabric, or 16 per FQ (see page 94). Cut 16 in GP 01-R, GP 02-J, GP 03-L, GP 04-L, GP 08-J and GP 09-L.
Backing:
Cut 2 pieces 45in x 62in (114cm x 157.5cm) in NS 01.
Straight cut binding:
Cut 7 strips 2½in- (6.5cm-) wide x width of fabric in NS 01, to form 7⅔yds (7m) of binding.

MAKING THE UNITS

Using a ¼in (6mm) seam allowance and following the block assembly, key and quilt assembly diagrams in strict order,

Storm At Sea
by Kaffe Fassett

unit assembly - Row A

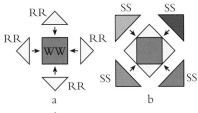

square unit

unit assembly - Row B

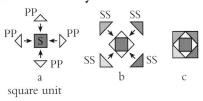

square unit

block assembly - Row A

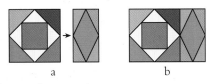

a   b

block assembly - Row B

a   b

make up 35 row A square units and 28 diamond units; and 24 row B square units and 30 diamond units.

Following the block assembly make up 28 row A blocks and 24 row B blocks. You should have 7 row A square units and 6 row B diamond units left over.

ASSEMBLING THE BLOCKS

Following the quilt assembly diagram in strict order, arrange 4 row A blocks in 7 rows with 1 of the remaining square units at the right hand end of each row. Arrange 4 row B blocks in 6 rows in between the A rows, with 1 of the remaining diamond units at the right hand end.

Using a ¼in (6mm) seam allowance, join the blocks into 13 rows. Then, join the rows together to form the quilt top. If you have assembled the quilt correctly you should see a wavy pattern forming, with red diagonal lines in one direction and green in the other.

FINISHING THE QUILT

Press assembled quilt top. Seam back pieces together with a ⅜in (1cm) seam allowance to form one piece approximately 62in x 86in (157cm x 218cm).

diamond unit
(Row A and Row B)

Layer the quilt top, batting and backing, and baste together (see page 98).

Using a toning thread, stitch-in-the-ditch diagonally up the wavy red sections, i.e. along the red sections of diamond blocks. Trim the quilt edges and attach the binding (see page 99).

Quilt assembly

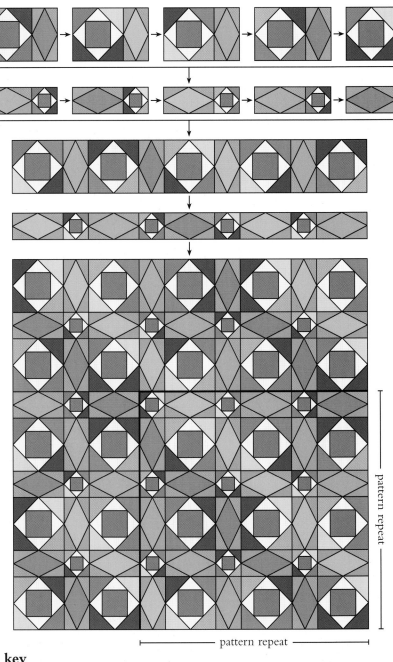

pattern repeat

pattern repeat

key

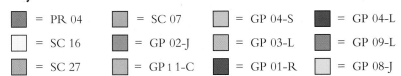

= PR 04	= SC 07	= GP 04-S	= GP 04-L
= SC 16	= GP 02-J	= GP 03-L	= GP 09-L
= SC 27	= GP 11-C	= GP 01-R	= GP 08-J

Autumn Garden
by Liza Prior Lucy
Instructions on page 40

Autumn Garden

LIZA PRIOR LUCY

When Liza Prior Lucy visited the Mac Kenzie Child store in New York, she saw a fabulous tiled floor, which inspired her to create this patchwork design. The result is this stunning large quilt, in rich autumnal colours, that is simple to construct in diagonal straight rows around the central square section. See page 16 for a paler version.

SIZE OF QUILT

The finished quilt will measure approximately 93½in x 93½in (238cm x 238cm).

MATERIALS

Patchwork fabrics:
GP 01-R: ¼yd (32cm) or 1FQ
GP 01-J: 1yd (90cm) or 5FQ
GP 02-J: ¼yd (32cm) or 1FQ
GP 03-J: ¼yd (32cm) or 1FQ
GP 04-J: See backing
GP 06-J: ⅛yd (15cm) or 1FQ
GP 07-J: ¼yd (32cm) or 1FQ
GP 08-J: ¼yd (32cm) or 1FQ
GP 09-J: ¼yd (32cm) or 1FQ
GP 11-C: 2⅔yds (2.4m) or 10FQ
PR 04: ¼yd (32cm) or 1FQ
NC 02: 1½yds (1.35m) or 6 FQ
NC 03: 1½yds (1.35m) or 6 FQ
Backing:
GP 04-J: 6½yds (5.85m)
Bias binding:
BS 08: ½yd (45cm)
Thin batting:
99½in x 99½in (253cm x 253cm)
Quilting thread:
Toning machine quilting thread.

Templates

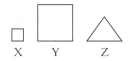

X   Y   Z

PATCH SHAPES

The quilt centre is made from one small square (template X). The edges of quilt centre and outer edges of the entire quilt are bordered by large triangles (template Z). The remainder of the quilt is formed by a large square (template Y). See pages 85 and 86 for templates.

CUTTING OUT

Template X: Cut 2⅝in- (6.7cm-) wide strips across width of fabric. Each strip will give you 16 patches per 45in- (114cm-) wide fabric, or 8 per FQ (see page 94).
Cut 10 in GP 06-J, 21 in PR 04, 23 in GP 04-J, 27 in GP 07-J, 30 in GP 01-R, 32 in GP 09-J, 33 in GP 08-J, 37 in GP 02-J and 43 in GP 03-J.
Template Z: Cut 6⅞in- (17.5cm-) wide strips across width of fabric. Each strip will give you 12 patches per 45in- (114cm-) wide fabric, or 6 per FQ.
Cut 60 in GP 01-J.
Template Y: Cut 6½in- (16.5cm-) wide strips across width of fabric. Each strip will give you 6 patches per 45in- (114cm-) wide fabric, or 3 per FQ.
Cut 48 in NC 02 and NC 03.
Fussy cut (see page 94) 84 in GP 11-C, centralising the flowers.
Backing:
Cut 2 pieces 45in x 99½in (114cm x 253cm) and 3 pieces 33½in x 12in (86cm x 30.5cm) in GP 04-J.
Bias binding:
Cut 10½yds (9.6m) of bias binding 2¼in- (6cm-) wide from BS 08.

MAKING THE QUILT CENTRE

Arrange 16 small square patches (template X) in 16 rows following the quilt assembly guide. Using a ¼in (6mm) seam allowance join the patches into 16 rows, then join the rows together to form the quilt centre.

COMPLETING THE QUILT TOP

To form the 4 triangular sections that fit the sides of the quilt centre, arrange 6 large squares (template Y) in 3 diagonal rows, edged with 4 large triangles (template Z) - see the quilt assembly diagram, right. Using a ¼in (6mm) seam allowance, assemble the rows and attach to quilt centre.
Using the quilt assembly diagram as a guide, make up the 4 large corner sections of the quilt, by arranging 6 rows of large squares (template Y) with a large triangle (template Z) at each end of the rows. Join rows together and seam the remaining large triangles together in 2's to form each corner. Join the made up sections to the quilt top in the order shown on the quilt assembly diagram, right.

FINISHING THE QUILT

Press the assembled quilt top and seam the 5 backing pieces together with a ⅜in (1cm) seam allowance to form one large piece approximately 99½in x 99½in (253cm x 253cm).
Layer the quilt top, batting and backing, and baste together (see page 98).
Free-motion quilt (see page 102) over the quilt centre in a very random fashion, working across 2 rows of small squares at one time. Loosely stitch around each flower shape on the large floral squares and free-motion quilt the remaining large squares in a very random fashion.
Trim the quilt edges level with the quilt top and attach the binding (see page 99).

Quilt assembly

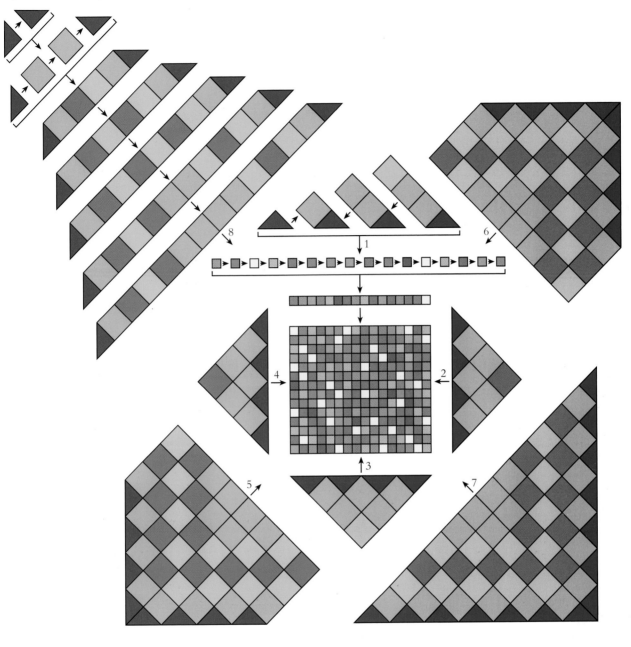

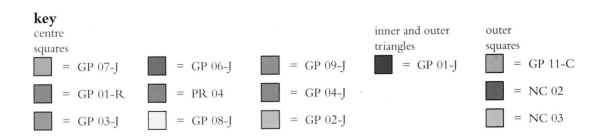

key

centre squares

▢ = GP 07-J	▢ = GP 06-J	▢ = GP 09-J	
▢ = GP 01-R	▢ = PR 04	▢ = GP 04-J	
▢ = GP 03-J	▢ = GP 08-J	▢ = GP 02-J	

inner and outer triangles

▢ = GP 01-J

outer squares

▢ = GP 11-C

▢ = NC 02

▢ = NC 03

Amish Indiana Baskets
by Roberta Horton

Amish Indiana Baskets

ROBERTA HORTON

Roberta is fascinated with the Amish people and their quilting designs. Indiana Baskets is a traditional design which for quickness, we hand-quilted this project with single rows of stitching; but for a more decorative effect, work double rows, spaced ¼in (6mm) apart, on the basket and border sections of the quilt. Turn to page 77, to find out more about Roberta's passion with the Amish.

SIZE OF QUILT
The finished quilt will measure approximately 57½in x 68½in (146cm x 174cm).

MATERIALS
Patchwork fabrics:
SC 02: ¼yd (23cm) or 1FQ
SC 03: ¼yd (23cm) or 1FQ
SC 04: ¼yd (23cm) or 1FQ
SC 05: ¼yd (23cm) or 1FQ
SC 06: ⅛yd (15cm) or 1FQ
SC 08: ¼yd (23cm) or 1FQ
SC 09: ¼yd (23cm) or 1FQ
SC 13: ½yd (45cm) or 2 FQ
SC 14: ⅔yd (60cm) or 2FQ
SC 15: ¼yd (23cm) or 1FQ
SC 20: ¼yd (23cm) or 1FQ
SC 21: ¼yd (23cm) or 1FQ
SC 23: ⅛yd (15cm) or 1FQ
SC 26: ¼yd (23cm) or 1FQ
SC 27: ¼yd (23cm) or 1FQ
SC 29: ⅛yd (15cm) or 1FQ
SC 31: ⅛yd (15cm) or 1FQ
SC 32: ⅛yd (15cm) or 1FQ
SC 36: ⅛yd (15cm) or 1FQ
Borders:
SC 25: see backing
Backing:
SC 25: 5¼yds (4.75m)
Straight cut binding:
SC 25: see backing
Batting:
64in x 74in (163cm x 188cm)
Quilting thread:
Black hand quilting thread

PATCH SHAPES
The quilt centre is made from 1 plain block 8½in x 8½in (21.5cm x 21.5cm) and 1 pieced block made from 11 tiny triangles (template QQ), 1 medium triangle (template U), 1 small triangle (template TT) and 2 rectangles (template T). The quilt centre is edged with 14 large triangles (template UU) and 4 medium triangles (template VV). See pages 83, 84, 89 and 90 for templates. You'll find half of template UU on page 90. Place fold edge of template UU to fold of paper. Trace around shape and cut out from double thickness paper. Open out for complete template.

Templates

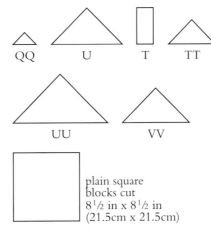

QQ   U   T   TT

UU   VV

plain square blocks cut 8½ in x 8½ in (21.5cm x 21.5cm)

CUTTING OUT
Template QQ: Cut 2⅞in- (7.3cm-) wide strips across width of fabric. Each strip will give you 30 patches per 45in- (114cm-) wide fabric, or 14 per FQ (see page 94). Cut 3 patches in SC 08, 4 in SC 27, 6 in SC 14 and SC 20, 8 in SC 02 and SC 21, 12 in SC 04, SC 06, SC 23 and SC 32, 13 in SC 09, 16 in SC 05, 24 in SC 29, SC 31 and SC 36, and 36 in SC 26.
Template TT: Cut 2 patches in SC 13, 4 in SC 03, SC 04, and SC 15, and 6 in SC 08.
Template T: Cut 4 patches in SC 13, 8 in SC 03, SC 04 and SC 15, and 12 in SC 08.
Template U: Cut 2 patches in SC 09 and SC 27, 4 in SC 02 and SC 21, and 8 in SC 05.
Template VV: Cut 4 in SC 14.
Template UU: Cut 14 in SC 14.
Plain square blocks: Cut 4 squares 8½in x 8½in (21.5cm x 21.5cm) in SC 20 and 8 in SC 13.
Borders:
Cut 2 side border 6½in x 56¾in (16.5cm x 144cm) and 2 end border 6½in x 57½in (16.5cm x 146cm) in SC 25.
Backing:
Cut 2 pieces of fabric for backing 37½in x 64in (95.2cm x 163cm) in SC 25.
Straight cut binding:
Cut 7¼yds (6.55m) of straight cut binding, 2½in (6.5cm) wide from SC 25.

MAKING THE PIECED BLOCKS
Using a ¼in (6mm) seam allowance, make up 20 pieced blocks using the key, block and quilt assembly diagrams as a guide (see pages 44 and 45).

ASSEMBLING THE BLOCKS
Arrange the 20 pieced blocks and 12 plain blocks alternately in 8 diagonal rows, with the large and medium triangles placed at the end of each row, as shown in the quilt assembly diagram. Using a ¼in (6mm) seam allowance, join the blocks together into rows, then join the rows together to form the quilt centre, adding the final 2 medium triangles to the remaining 2 diagonal corners.

Quilt assembly

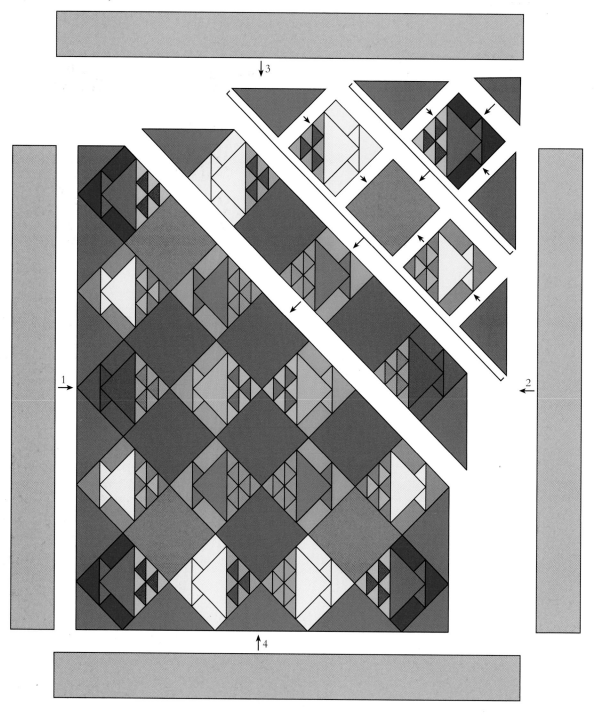

key

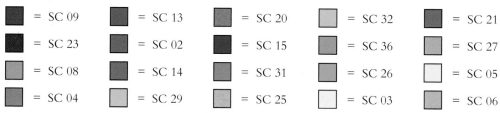

■ = SC 09		■ = SC 13		■ = SC 20		■ = SC 32		■ = SC 21
■ = SC 23		■ = SC 02		■ = SC 15		■ = SC 36		■ = SC 27
■ = SC 08		■ = SC 14		■ = SC 31		■ = SC 26		■ = SC 05
■ = SC 04		■ = SC 29		■ = SC 25		■ = SC 03		■ = SC 06

Pieced block assembly
Top unit assembly

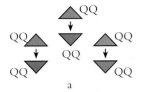

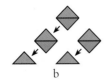

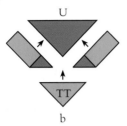

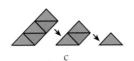

Basket unit assembly

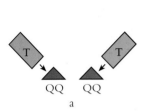

Block assembly

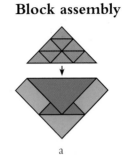

Quilting diagram
pieced blocks

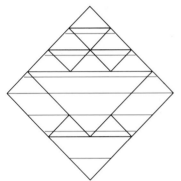

Quilting diagram
plain blocks

ATTACHING THE BORDERS

Using a ¼in (6mm) seam allowance, attach the 2 side borders and then the end borders to the quilt edges.

FINISHING THE QUILT

Press the assembled quilt top. Seam the 2 backing pieces together with a ⅜in (1cm) seam allowance to form 1 piece approximately 64in x 74in (163cm x 188cm). Layer the quilt top, batting and backing, and baste together (see page 98). Using the large quilting diagram as a guide, hand quilt the plain centre blocks. Work 6 with 11 parallel rows of stitching spaced evenly apart, then work another 11 rows in the opposite direction to cross at 90 degrees. Work the centre top and bottom plain blocks with 6 chevron rows of quilting spaced evenly apart. On the remaining 4 plain blocks work 7 parallel rows spaced evenly apart. See separate small diagram for quilting the pieced blocks. Finally to quilt the borders, work diagonal rows of parallel stitching at a 45 degree angle to the quilt edges, spaced approximately 1½in (4cm) apart, so that they form a right angle to each other at the border seams (see large diagram).

Trim the quilt edges and attach the binding (see page 99).

Wagga Wagga

BRANDON MABLY

The Power House in Sydney, Australia's captial city, displays one of the most handsome collections of traditional 'Wagga Wagga' quilts in the world. They were made by the first European settlers in Australia, from subtle contrasting blocks of men's suiting fabrics. The faded colours of Rowan's shot cottons have allowed Brandon to create a very similar effect.

SIZE OF QUILT

The finished quilt will measure approximately 64¼in x 93½in (163cm x 238cm).

MATERIALS

Patchwork fabrics:
SC 03: ⅓yd (30cm) or 2FQ
SC 04: ½yd (45cm) or 2FQ
SC 06: ½yd (45cm) or 2FQ
SC 15: ½yd (45cm) or 2FQ
SC 16: ¼yd (23cm) or 1FQ
SC 17: ⅔yd (60cm) or 3FQ
SC 18: ⅛yd (15cm) or 1FQ
SC 19: ¾yd (70cm) or 2FQ
SC 20: ½yd (45cm) or 2FQ
SC 22: ⅓yd (30cm) or 2FQ
SC 23: ⅓yd (30cm) or 2FQ
SC 24: ¾yd (70cm) or 3FQ
SC 25: ½yd (45cm) or 2FQ
SC 29: ½yd (45cm) or 2FQ
SC 31: see binding

Backing:
RS 04: 5yds (4.5m)

Straight cut binding:
SC 31: 1yd (90cm)

Batting:
70in x 100in (178cm x 254cm)

Quilting thread:
Terracotta Rowan Cotton Glacé

Templates

Q   MM

PATCH SHAPES

The main part of the quilt is made from one small square (template Q), and bordered around the edges with a small triangle (template MM). See pages 83 and 88 for templates.

CUTTING OUT

Template Q: Cut 3½in- (9cm-) wide strips across width of fabric. Each strip will give you 12 patches per 45in- (114cm-) wide fabric, or 6 per FQ (see page 94).
Cut 31 in SC 03, 34 in SC 23, 36 in SC 20, 37 in SC 22 and SC 31, 43 in SC 04, 46 in SC 25, 47 in SC 19, 53 in SC 06, 57 in SC 29, 59 in SC 15, 70 in SC 17 and 73 in SC 24.

Template MM: Cut 3⅞in- (9.9cm-) wide strips across width of fabric. Each strip will give you 22 patches per 45in- (114cm-) wide fabric, or 10 per FQ (see page 94).
Cut 10 in SC 19, 16 in SC 18, 20 in SC 31 and 28 in SC 16.

Backing:
Cut 2 pieces 45in x 70in (114cm x 178cm) and 2 pieces 12in x 35¼in (30.5cm x 89.5cm) in RS 04.

Straight cut binding:
Cut 8 strips 2½in- (6.5cm-) wide x width of fabric in SC 31, to form 9yds (8.10m) of binding.

ASSEMBLING THE QUILT

Following the key and quilt assembly diagram in strict order (see page 48), arrange 36 diagonal rows of square patches with a triangular patch at each end. Make sure grainlines on the square patches run in the same direction to avoid shading, when adjacent squares of the same colour are seamed together.
Using a ¼in (6mm) seam allowance join the patches into rows, and then join the rows together to form the quilt top.

FINISHING THE QUILT

Press the assembled quilt top. Seam the 4 backing fabric pieces together with a ⅜in (1cm) seam allowance to form one large piece approximately 70in x 100in (178cm x 254cm).
Layer the quilt top, batting and backing, and baste together (see page 98).
Using the cotton glacé, handstitch ⅜in (1cm) crosses ay the position where the seams bisect on the dark coloured rows to tie the quilt layers together (see quilting diagram below).
Trim the quilt edges and attach the binding (see page 99).

Quilting

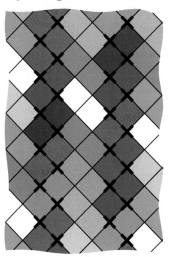

Wagga Wagga
by Brandon Mably

Quilt assembly

key

centre squares

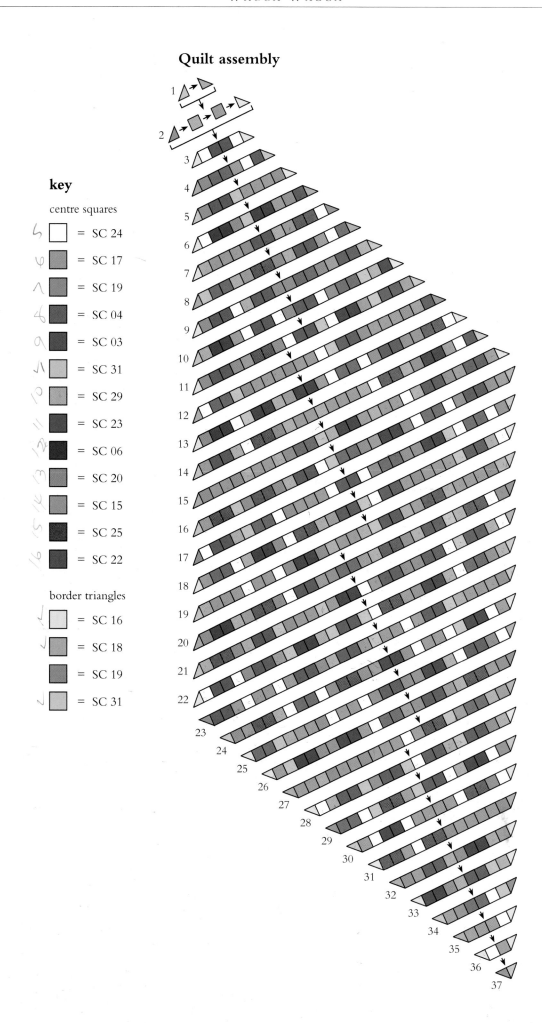

= SC 24

= SC 17

= SC 19

= SC 04

= SC 03

= SC 31

= SC 29

= SC 23

= SC 06

= SC 20

= SC 15

= SC 25

= SC 22

border triangles

= SC 16

= SC 18

= SC 19

= SC 31

Dark Bob's Your Uncle
by Kaffe Fassett
Instructions on page 50

Dark Bob's Your Uncle

KAFFE FASSETT

This very rich version of the Bob's Your Uncle Quilt was inspired by an African beaded bag. It is a very textural project - not only does it have the wonderful combinations of colours and fabrics, but Kaffe has used surface decoration in the form of narrow ribbons and buttons to enhance the edges and centres of each block. Also see page 6 for a pale version of this quilt.

SIZE OF QUILT

The finished quilt will measure approximately 42in x 50½in (107cm x 128cm).

MATERIALS

Patchwork fabrics:
SC 19: ¼yd (23cm) or 1FQ
GP 01-L: ⅛yd (15cm) or 1FQ
GP 01-R: ⅛yd (15cm) or 1FQ
GP 01-G: ⅛yd (15cm) or 1FQ
GP 01-BW: ⅛yd (15cm) or 1FQ
GP 02-J: ⅛yd (15cm) or 1FQ
GP 03-J: See border corners
GP 04-J: ⅛yd (15cm) or 1FQ
GP 04-L: ⅛yd (15cm) or 1FQ
GP 04-C: ⅛yd (15cm) or 1FQ
GP 06-J: See backing
GP 07-J: ⅛yd (15cm) or 1FQ
GP 07-L: ⅛yd (15cm) or 1FQ
GP 07-C: ⅛yd (15cm) or 1FQ
PR 02: ⅛yd (15cm) or 1FQ
PR 05: ⅛yd (15cm) or 1FQ
PR 07: ⅛yd (15cm) or 1FQ
ES 20: ½yd (45cm) or 2FQ

Outer borders:
GP 08-J: ⅔yd (60cm)

Border corners:
GP 03-J: ¼yd (23cm) or 1FQ

Backing:
GP 06-J: 1⅔yd (1.5m)

Bias binding:
NS 17: ¼yd (23cm)

Batting:
48in x 56in (122cm x 142cm)

Petersham ribbon:
17¾yds (16m) of ¼in- (6mm-) wide Petersham ribbon

Buttons:
36 2-hole ½in (1.2mm) buttons in a selection of red, blue and green

Templates

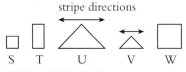

stripe directions

S   T   U   V   W

PATCH SHAPES

The quilt centre is made from a small square (template S) and a rectangle (template T). The edges of the centre are bordered by large triangles (template U), with small triangles at the corners (template V). There are straight outer borders, with a large square at each corner (template W). See page 82, 83 and 84 for templates.

CUTTING OUT

Template S: Cut 2½in- (6.5cm-) wide strips across width of fabric. Each strip will give you 18 patches per 45in- (114cm-) wide fabric, or 8 per FQ (see page 94). Cut 32 in SC 19.

Template T: Cut 8 in GP 01-L, GP 01-BW, GP 01-R, GP 01-G, GP 02-J, GP 03-J, GP 04-J, GP 04-L, GP 04-C, GP 06-J, GP 07-C, GP 07-L, GP 07-J, PR 02, PR 05 and PR 07.

Template U: Cut 14 in ES 20.

Template V: Cut 8 in ES 20.

Template W: Cut 4 in GP 03-J.

Outer borders:
Cut 2 side borders 4½in x 34½in (11.5cm x 87.5cm) and 2 end borders 4½in x 43in (11.5cm x 109cm) in GP 08-J.

Backing:
Cut 1 piece 45in x 56in (114cm x 142cm) in GP 06-J.

Bias binding:
Cut 5¼yds (4.75m) of bias binding 2¼in- (6cm-) wide from NS 17.

Block assembly

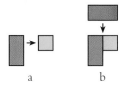

a   b

c   d

MAKING THE BLOCKS

Using a ¼in (6mm) seam allowance make up 8 A blocks, 8 B blocks, 8 C blocks and 8 D blocks using the quilt assembly key as a guide and stitching between the dots only. When inserting the last patch into each block use the inset seam technique (see page 96).

ASSEMBLING THE BLOCKS

Arrange the 32 blocks and 14 large triangles into 8 diagonal rows following the quilt assembly diagram, opposite. Using a ¼in (6mm) seam allowance, join the blocks together into rows, then join the rows together to form the quilt top. Join 2 small triangles together for each corner of the quilt centre and stitch to each of the corners.

MAKING THE OUTER BORDERS

Using a ¼in (6mm) seam allowance, attach the 2 side borders to the quilt edges. Join a corner square (template W) to each end of the end borders and attach to the quilt edges.

Quilt assembly

key

block A

block B

block C

block D

= GP 02-J	= GP 03-J	= GP 01-R	= GP 07-J
= GP 01-L	= GP 07-L	= GP 04-L	= PR 05
= GP 04-J	= GP 06-J	= PR 02	= GP 01-G
= PR 07	= GP 01-BW	= GP 07-C	= GP 04-C

block centres, borders and outer triangles

= SC 19	= GP 08-J	= GP 03-J	= ES 20	▬ = ribbon trim

FINISHING THE QUILT

Press the assembled quilt top. Layer the quilt top, batting and backing, and baste together (see page 98).

Using the quilt assembly diagram as a guide, stitch a length of Petersham ribbon along the edges of each row of blocks in both directions. Then, stitch a length of ribbon around the inner edges of the outer border, covering the raw ends of the other pieces of ribbon.

Trim the quilt edges and attach the binding (see page 99). Finally, hand stitch a button to the centre of each block, placing the different colours at random.

51

Nine Patch Striped Bag

Pauline Smith

This pretty bag with long shoulder straps is based on the Nine Patch Quilt (see page 23), but Pauline has chosen a richer colour palette for this project. The front of the bag could easily be turned into a cushion, or enlarged to make a great floor cushion. Turn to page 101 in the Patchwork Know How for full instructions on completing a cushion.

SIZE OF BAG
The finished bag will measure approx 18½in x 18½in (47cm x 47cm).

MATERIALS
Patchwork fabrics:
SC 01: See back bag strips
SC 06: See inner borders
SC 07: ⅛yd (15cm) or 1FQ
SC 08: See back bag strips
SC 09: See back bag strips
SC 18: ⅛yd (15cm) or 1FQ
SC 20: ⅛yd (15cm) or 1FQ
PS 05: See straps
Inner borders:
SC 06: ¼yd (23cm) or 1FQ
SC 15: ¼yd (23cm) or 1FQ
Back bag strips:
SC 01: ⅛yd (15cm) or 1FQ
SC 08: ⅔yd (60cm) or 2FQ
SC 09: ⅔yd (60cm) or 2FQ
Straps:
SC 09: See back bag strips
PS 05: ⅓yd (30cm) or 1FQ
Lining:
SC 08: See back bag strips
SC 09: See back bag strips
Batting:
¾yd (70cm) x 45in (114cm) wide
Quilting thread:
Toning machine quilting thread.

Templates

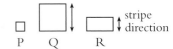

P   Q   R   stripe direction

PATCH SHAPES
The bag front is made up of a nine patch pieced block (template P), stitched

together in rows with rectangular blocks (template R) and square blocks (template Q). See pages 82 and 83 for templates. The rows are then joined together alternately with inner borders. The bag back is made up of alternating strips and inner borders.

CUTTING OUT

Template P: Cut 8 in SC 01, 9 in SC 07, 11 in SC 08, 12 in SC 09, 13 in SC 20, 14 in SC 06 and SC 18.

Template Q: Cut 6 in PS 05.

Template R: Cut 6 in PS 05.

Inner borders:
Cut 4 inner borders 3in x 19in (7.5cm x 48cm) in SC 06 and SC 15.

Back bag strips:
Cut 1 strip 3½in x 19in (9cm x 48cm) in SC 01, SC 08 and SC 09.

Straps:
Cut 4 pieces 3¾in x 15½in (9.5cm x 39.5cm) in SC 09 and PS 05 with stripes running across the straps.

Lining:
Cut 1 piece 19in x 19in (48cm x 48cm) in SC 08 and SC 09.

Batting:
Cut 2 pieces 19in x 19in (48cm x 48cm) for the front and back and 2 pieces 3¾in x 30½in (9.5cm x 77.5cm) for the straps.

Block assembly

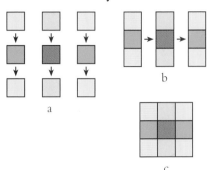

a

b

c

MAKING THE NINE PATCH BLOCKS

Using a ¼in (6mm) seam allowance, make up 9 blocks, using the block and bag front assembly diagrams as a guide.

MAKING THE BAG FRONT

Using a ¼in (6mm) seam allowance, assemble 3 rows of 3 nine patch blocks alternating with 2 square blocks (template Q) and a rectangular block (template R) at each end. Use the bag front assembly diagram as a guide.

Arrange the pieced rows alternately with 4 inner borders following the bag front assembly diagram. Using a ¼in (6mm) seam allowance, join the rows and borders together form the bag front.

MAKING THE BAG BACK

Arrange the remaining 4 inner borders alternately with the 3 back bag strips. Using a ¼in (6mm) seam allowance, join the strips and borders together form the bag back.

QUILTING THE FRONT AND BACK

Press the assembled front and back bag quilt tops.

Layer the quilt top and batting, and baste together (see page 98). Using a toning thread, stitch-in-the-ditch down each row (see page 102). Trim the quilt edges.

FINISHING OFF THE BAG

For full instructions on how to complete the bag, turn to page 99 in the Patchwork know-how section.

key

▨	= SC 07
▨	= SC 08
▨	= SC 20
▨	= SC 01
▨	= SC 09
▨	= SC 18
▨	= SC 06
▨	= SC 15
▨	= PS 05

Bag front assembly

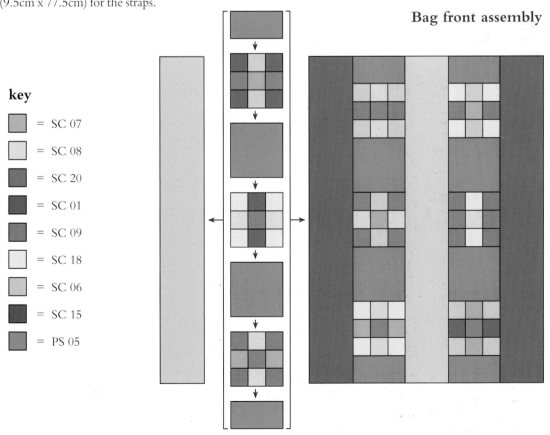

CLEAN LIVING

Twelve contemporary designs, using a mix of clear bright colours – think of
East meets West with a touch of Zen blended with modern art, geometrics
and absolutely no fuss

Willow Table Runner

KIM HARGREAVES

With this project and the following five: Chime Bag, Blossom Bag and the four different cushion styles, Kim wanted to produce simple contemporary designs that would sit equally well in both modern and more traditional settings. In essence these designs are really appliqué projects, as the decoration is formed by stitching on square patches.

SIZE OF TABLE RUNNER
The finished table runner will measure approximately 16½in x 82in (42cm x 208cm).

MATERIALS
Appliqué fabrics:
SC 03: ⅛yd (15cm) or 1FQ
SC 19: ⅛yd (15cm) or 1FQ
SC 29: ⅛yd (15cm) or 1FQ
Runner fabric:
SC 31: 2⅓yds (2.2m)
Centre band fabric:
SC 25: ⅓yd (30cm)
Paper-backed adhesive web:
½yd (45cm) x 35½in (90cm) wide
Appliqué threads:
Matching machine threads

PATCH SHAPES
The appliqué on this table runner is formed from 3 sizes of square: 1in (2.5cm), 1½in (4cm) and 2in (5cm).

CUTTING OUT
Main runner:
Cut 1 rectangular piece 34in x 83in (86.5 x 211cm) in SC 31.
Centre band:
Cut 2 strips 5½in x 41⅞in (14cm x 104cm) in SC 25.
Appliqué squares:
Iron the adhesive web on to the reverse side of the appliqué fabrics and cut a selection of the different square sizes from the various colours.

MAKING UP THE RUNNER
Fold the main runner in half along its length and using a ⅜in (1cm) seam allowance, stitch the long edges together.

Press seam open. Turn through to right side and refold runner so seam runs up the centre on one side. Press flat.

APPLIQUEING THE RUNNER
Join the 2 centre band strips to form 1 long strip. Press seam open. Iron the remaining adhesive web on to the wrong side, making sure it is completely covered.

Peel off the paper backing and position the band over the central seam on the runner. Press the raw open edges of the runner ½in (1.2cm) to the wrong side and slipstitch the open end edges closed. Machine-appliqué the central band in place (see page 97). Arrange the assorted squares along the central band and machine-appliqué in place.

Cushions

KIM HARGREAVES

SIZE OF CUSHIONS

The finished cushions will measure approximately 17½in x 17½in (44.5cm x 44.5cm).

MATERIALS

Breeze Cushion (below):
Appliqué fabrics:
SC 25: see cushion backs
SC 29: see cushion front
Cushion front:
SC 29: ⅔yd (60cm) or 2FQ
Cushion backs:
SC 25: ½yd (45cm) or 2FQ
Lightweight iron-on interfacing:
⅔yd (60cm) x 35½in (90cm) wide
Paper-backed adhesive web:
¼yd (23cm) x 35½in (90cm) wide
Cushion pad:
18in x 18in (45cm x 45cm)
Appliqué thread:
Matching machine thread

Lang Cushion (opposite right):
Appliqué fabrics:
SC 02: remnant
SC 19: remnant
SC 25: remnant
SC 31: remnant
Cushion front and back:
SC 29: ⅔yd (60cm) or 3FQ
Paper-backed adhesive web:
⅛yd (15cm) x 35½in (90cm) wide
Cushion pad:
18in x 18in (45cm x 45cm)
Appliqué thread:
Matching machine threads

Air Cushion (opposite left):
Appliqué fabrics:
SC 03: remnant
SC 19: remnant
SC 31: remnant
Cushion front and back:
SC 29: ⅔yd (60cm) or 3FQ
Front band:
SC 25: ¼yd (23cm) or 1FQ
Paper-backed adhesive web:
¼yd (23cm) x 35½in (90cm) wide
Cushion pad:
18in x 18in (45cm x 45cm)
Appliqué thread:
Matching machine threads

Bamboo Cushion (see page 64):
Appliqué fabrics:
SC 01: remnant
SC 02: remnant
SC 16: remnant
Cushion front and back:
SC 25: ⅔yd (60cm) or 3FQ
Front bands:
SC 19: ¼yd (23cm) or 1FQ
Paper-backed adhesive web:
¼yd (23cm) x 35½in (90cm) wide
Cushion pad:
18in x 18in (45cm x 45cm)
Appliqué thread:
Matching machine threads

PATCH SHAPES

The appliqué on these cushions is formed from squares of various sizes: 1in (2.5cm), 1½in (4cm), 2in (5cm), 2¾in (7cm), and 4in (10cm).

CUTTING OUT

Cushion pieces:
For each cushion cut:
1 cushion front 18½in x 18½in (47cm x 47cm),
1 small cushion back 11in x 18½in (28cm x 47cm)
1 large cushion back 15¾in x 18½in (40cm x 47cm).

Air cushion front band:
Iron adhesive web to the wrong side of SC 25 and cut a strip 5¾in x 18½in (14.5cm x 47cm).

Bamboo cushion front bands:
Iron adhesive web to the wrong side of SC 19 and cut 2 strips 5in x 13½in (12.5cm x 34cm).
Appliqué squares:
Iron adhesive web to the reverse side of the appliqué fabric scraps.
Breeze cushion appliqué squares: cut 41 x 2in (5cm) and 40 x 1in (2.5cm) squares from SC 25. Cut 41 x 1in (2.5cm) squares from SC 29.
Lang cushion appliqué squares: cut 1 square from each of the different coloured appliqué fabrics, making each a different size.
Air cushion appliqué squares: cut 2 or 3 x 1in (2.5cm) squares and 1 or 2 x 1½in (4cm) squares from each appliqué fabric.
Bamboo cushion appliqué squares: cut 1 x 1in (2.5cm) in SC 02 and SC 16, and 14 in SC 01.

APPLIQUÉING CUSHION FRONTS

Breeze cushion: Press interfacing to the wrong side of the front cushion and machine-appliqué first the large squares and then the small squares to the front in a chequer-board fashion as shown for the Blossom bag (see page 58).
Lang cushion: Machine-appliqué patches to the centre of the front cushion (see page 97), layering them one on top of the other and setting them at slightly different angles.
Air cushion: Machine-appliqué the front band to the cushion front and arrange the squares along the band mixing the sizes, colours and positions. Machine-appliqué in place.
Bamboo cushion: Machine-appliqué the 2 front bands to the front cushion. Arrange half the squares in a line along each front band, mixing in 1 odd colour on each band. Machine-appliqué in place.

FINISHING OFF THE CUSHIONS

For full instructions on how to complete the cushions, turn to page 101 in the Patchwork know-how section.

Air, Breeze and Lang Cushions
by Kim Hargreaves
Instructions on page 56

Blossom Bag

KIM HARGREAVES

SIZE OF BAG
The finished bag will measure approximately 10in x 10in (25.5cm x 25.5cm).

MATERIALS
Appliqué fabrics:
SC 03: ⅛yd (15cm) or 1FQ
SC 29: ⅛yd (15cm) or 1FQ
Main bag fabric:
SC 31: ⅓yd (30cm) or 1FQ
Lining:
SC 25: ⅓yd (30cm) or 1FQ
Lightweight iron-on interfacing:
⅓yd (30cm) x 35½in (90cm) wide
Paper-backed adhesive web:
½yd (45cm) x 35½in (90cm) wide
Thick piping cord:
10¼in (26cm) of ⅜in- (10mm-) thick cord
Appliqué thread:
Contrasting grey machine thread

PATCH SHAPES
The appliqué on this bag is formed from 3 sizes of square: ¾in (2cm), 1½in (4cm) and 2in (5cm).

CUTTING OUT
Main Bag:
From SC 31 and iron-on interfacing cut: a front and back bag 10¾in x 10¾in (27.3cm x 27.3cm); 2 side gussets and 1 base gusset 3¾in x 10¾in (9.5cm x 27.3cm); a front and back facing 10¾in x 1½in (27.3cm x 4cm) and 2 side gusset facings 1½in x 3¾in (4cm x 9.5cm).
Lining:
From SC 25 cut: a front and back bag lining 10in x 10¾in (25.5cm x 27.3cm); 2 side gusset linings 3¾in x 10in (9.5cm x 25.5cm), and 1 base gusset lining 3¾in x 10¾in (9.5cm x 27.3cm). Retain some of this colour (SC 25) for the bias strips for the bag handles (see Step 4 of Completing the Blossom Bag in the Patchwork Know-how, on page 100).
Appliqué squares:
Divide the adhesive web into 3 equal quantities and iron a piece on to the reverse side of the fabric SC 03, SC 29 and remaining SC 25. From SC 29 cut 26 x 2in (5cm) squares; from SC 03 cut 26 x 1½in (4cm) squares, and from SC 25 cut 26 x ¾in (2cm) squares.

APPLIQUÉING FRONT AND BACK BAGS
Press interfacing to the wrong side of the front and back bag pieces.
Using a chalk marker, draw the seam allowance position around each side of the front and back bags, ⅜in (1cm) in from the edges.
Arrange the 2in (5cm) squares on to the right side of the front and back bags, within the drawn lines, in a chequer-board fashion.
Peel the paper backing from each of the squares, making sure you place them back in the original position, and machine appliqué the shapes in place (see page 97). Repeat with the other 2 sizes of square, letting the squares sit at various angles within the other squares. Don't be tempted to line them all up exactly - the haphazard arrangement is part of the joy of this design.

FINISHING OFF THE BAG
For full instructions on how to complete the bag, turn to page 100 in the Patchwork know-how section.

Chime Bag

KIM HARGREAVES

SIZE OF BAG
The finished bag will measure approximately 9¼in x 13½in (23.5cm x 34cm).

MATERIALS
Appliqué and bag fabric:
SC 29: ½yd (45cm) or 2FQ
Paper-backed adhesive web:
⅛yd (15cm) x 35½in (90cm) wide
Thin piping cord:
15¾in (40cm) x ¼in (6mm) beige cord
Appliqué thread:
Matching and contrasting machine threads

PATCH SHAPES
The appliqué on this bag is formed from 2 sizes of square: 1in (2.5cm) and 1½in (4cm).

CUTTING OUT
Bag sides and lining:
For the bag cut 2 bag pieces and 2 lining pieces 10in x 14½in (25.5cm x 37cm).

Appliqué squares:
Iron the adhesive web on to the reverse side of the remaining fabric and cut 41 x 1in (2.5cm) squares and 3 x 1½in (4cm).

APPLIQUÉING THE BAG
Arrange the 1in (2.5cm) squares on to the right side of front bag in 6 rows of 6 and machine-appliqué them in position using a mixture of the matching and contrasting threads (see page 97). Arrange the remaining squares in a random fashion on the back bag and appliqué in place as before.

FINISHING OFF THE BAG
For full instructions on how to complete the bag, turn to page 101 in the Patchwork know-how section.

Blossom Bag
by Kim Hargreaves

Chime Bag by Kim Hargreaves
Instructions on page 58

Jupiter Sunset

SANDRA TOWNSEND DONABED

This stunning quilt is worked in the same free-hand foundation-piecing method as Liza's Chinese Coins and Log Cabins (page 65), but using the colours combined in groups, creates a very dramatic radiating effect. This design is easy to size up and down. Make 24 blocks for a single bed, 36 for a double, and 64 for a king size (fabric quantities below are for 16 blocks - adjust them accordingly).

SIZE OF QUILT

The finished quilt will measure approx 57½in x 57½in (146cm x 146cm).

MATERIALS

Patchwork fabrics:
(All quantities are approximate)
Accent colours:
SC 02: ⅛yd (15cm) or 1FQ
SC 07: ⅛yd (15cm) or 1FQ
SC 08: ⅛yd (15cm) or 1FQ
SC 09: ⅛yd (15cm) or 1FQ
SC 10: ⅛yd (15cm) or 1FQ
SC 11: ⅛yd (15cm) or 1FQ
Light colours:
SC 05: ⅛yd (15cm) or 1FQ
SC 14: ¼yd (23cm) or 1FQ
SC 16: ⅛yd (15cm) or 1FQ
SC 17: ⅛yd (15cm) or 1FQ
SC 19: ¼yd (23cm) or 1FQ
SC 24: ¼yd (23cm) or 1FQ
SC 26: ¼yd (23cm) or 1FQ
SC 27: ⅛yd (15cm) or 1FQ
Medium colours:
SC 01: ⅛yd (15cm) or 1FQ
SC 12: ¼yd (23cm) or 1FQ
SC 18: ¼yd (23cm) or 1FQ
SC 19: See light colours
SC 20: ¼yd (23cm) or 1FQ
SC 21: ¼yd (23cm) or 1FQ
SC 22: ¼yd (23cm) or 1FQ
SC 23: ¼yd (23cm) or 1FQ
Dark colours:
SC 03: ¼yd (23cm) or 1FQ
SC 04: ¼yd (23cm) or 1FQ
SC 06: ⅓yd (30cm) or 1FQ
SC 13: See borders and bias binding
SC 15: ⅓yd (30cm) or 1FQ
SC 25: ¼yd (23cm) or 1FQ
Borders and bias binding:
SC 13: 1⅓yds (1.2m)

Backing:
BC 04: 2½yds (2.25m)
Batting:
60in x 60in (152.5cm x 152.5cm) very fine flannel
Quilting thread:
Dark toning machine quilting thread

Foundation blocks

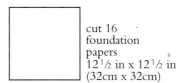

cut 16 foundation papers 12½ in x 12½ in (32cm x 32cm)

FOUNDATION PAPERS

The quilt centre is made up of 1 free-hand foundation block. Cut 16 foundation papers 12½in x 12½in (32cm x 32cm) - see page 95.
You will find an example of a 50 percent foundation block printed at the back of this book to use as a stitching guide (see page 93).

CUTTING OUT

Inner borders:
Cut 4 side border strips 2in x 24½in (5cm x 62.5cm) and 4 end border strips 2in x 26in (5cm x 66cm) in SC 13.
Pieced borders:
Cut 2 strips 2in (5cm) wide across width of fabric in SC 13. Cut up strips into lengths of 2 - 5in (5 - 12.5cm).
Outer borders:
Cut 4 side border strips 2in x 27½in (5cm x 70cm) and 4 end border strips 2in x 29in (5cm x 74cm) in SC 13.
Straight cut binding:
Cut 6½yds (5.85m) of straight cut binding 2¼in (6cm) wide from SC 13.

Foundation patches:
Cut all the light, medium and dark coloured patchwork fabrics into rough strips across the width of the fabric, making them anything from 1½in (4cm) to 4in (10cm) wide. See page 95 (cutting foundation patches for free-hand blocks). Cut 20 block corners, free-hand, from all the accent colours (except SC 11). Cut them in somewhat trapezoidal shapes avoiding 90 degree angles, approximately 3 - 4in (7.5 - 10cm) on each side. Free-hand cut 3 strips across width of fabric roughly 1in (2.5cm) wide from SC 11.
Backing:
Cut 1 piece 45in x 60in (114cm x 152cm), and 2 pieces 16in x 30¼in (40.5cm x 77cm) in BC 04.

MAKING THE FOUNDATION BLOCKS

Set aside 4 foundation papers and 4 accent block corners for the centre blocks. Then, pin 1 accent block corner to each of the remaining foundation papers, letting the edges overhang slightly. Following a sort of free-hand half Log Cabin method (see page 96), attach a strip of SC 11 to the 2 inner raw edges of each corner block.
Continue working out from the corner attaching the light colours, but make sure you never have the same colour on both sides of the square. Work until you have reached the centre of the foundation paper, then start using the medium colours, until two-thirds of the paper is covered. Finally, complete the blocks using the dark colours.
Trim the edges of the fabric flush with the foundation patches.

MAKING THE CENTRE FOUNDATION BLOCKS

Make up the 4 remaining foundation blocks as before. Then, take the set aside accent block corners, and sew an SC 11 strip to 2 adjoining sides. Press under a $^{1}/_{4}$in (6mm) hem along the raw edges of the SC 11 strips. Keeping raw edges level, baste 1 to each of the 4 foundation blocks, on the corners diagonally opposite the existing accent block corners. Hand appliqué them in place around the pressed edges (see page 97), and stitch-in-the-ditch (see page 102) around the inner edges of the corner blocks. Trim away the foundation patches from under the appliqué to reduce bulk.

ASSEMBLING THE BLOCKS

Arrange the foundation blocks in 4 sets of 4 with the accent-coloured corners all facing towards the centre of each '4-patch' block and the appliquéd corners all facing towards what will be the centre of the quilt (see the quilt assembly diagram). Using a $^{1}/_{4}$in (6mm) seam allowance, join the blocks together into the 4 groups of 4. Then, join them into 2 groups of 8, and finally the 2 sets together to form the quilt centre with the appliquéd corners all meeting in the middle.

MAKING THE INNER BORDERS

Using a $^{1}/_{4}$in (6mm) seam allowance, join the side borders to form 2 strips, 48$^{1}/_{2}$in (122cm) long, and the end borders to form 2 strips, 51$^{1}/_{2}$in (131cm) long. Attach the 2 side borders to the edges of the quilt, and then attach the end borders.

MAKING THE PIECED BORDERS

Take any leftover tails from the many coloured strips and cut them into 2in (5cm) pieces, regardless of what the other side measures. Alternating the coloured strips with the pieced border

strips cut from SC 13, join the pieces to form 2 side borders, 2in wide x 51$^{1}/_{2}$in (5cm wide x 131cm) long, and 2 end borders, 2in wide x 54$^{1}/_{2}$in (5cm wide x 138.5cm) long. Attach the side borders to the edges of the quilt, then attach the end borders.

MAKING THE OUTER BORDERS

Using a $^{1}/_{4}$in (6mm) seam allowance, join the side borders to form 2 strips, 54$^{1}/_{2}$in (138.5cm) long, and the end borders to form 2 strips, 57$^{1}/_{2}$in (146cm) long. Attach the 2 side borders to the edges of the quilt, and then attach the end borders.

FINISHING THE WALL HANGING

Press the assembled quilt top. Seam the 3 backing pieces together with a $^{3}/_{8}$in (1cm) seam allowance to form one piece approximately 60in x 60in (152.5cm x 152.5cm).

Layer the quilt top, batting and backing, and baste together (see page 98).

To work the quilting design, use a large dinner plate to mark circles on the right side of the quilt (see page 97). Start by marking a full circle in the centre with further overlapping circles radiating out like petals. Mark a full circle in each corner of quilt and half circles, edge to edge around the sides of the quilt, overlapping at the corners. Machine quilt the circles in place. Trim the quilt edges and attach the binding (see page 99).

Turn to page 101 in the Patchwork know-how section for instructions on how to prepare a patchwork for hanging.

key

■	= SC 09	■	= SC 10
■	= SC 07	□	= SC 11
■	= SC 02	■	= SC 13

Quilt assembly

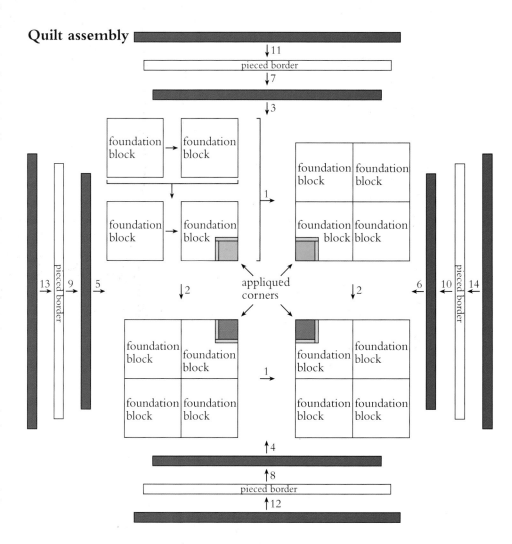

Jupiter Sunset
by Sandra Townsend Donabed
Instructions on page 61

Chinese Coins & Log Cabin by Liza Prior Lucy and
Bamboo Cushion by Kim Hargreaves Instructions on page 56

Chinese Coins & Log Cabin

LIZA PRIOR LUCY

Worked on foundation papers, the blocks in this quilt are formed with wiggly-cut strips of fabric it's a great design for using up all those odd remnants. We've given you four blocks at the back of the book as a guide, but the best approach is to simply lay out fabric strips in a way that appeals to you, and then start stitching. There are no rules, just enjoy and have fun.

SIZE OF QUILT
The finished quilt will measure approx 48in x 56in (122cm x 142cm).

MATERIALS
Patchwork fabrics:
(All quantities are approximate)
SC 01: $\frac{1}{8}$yd (15cm) or 1FQ
SC 02: $\frac{1}{8}$yd (15cm) or 1FQ
SC 05: $\frac{1}{8}$yd (15cm) or 1FQ
SC 07: $\frac{1}{8}$yd (15cm) or 1FQ
SC 08: $\frac{1}{4}$yd (23cm) or 1FQ
SC 10: Optional
SC 11: $\frac{1}{8}$yd (15cm) or 1FQ
SC 12: $\frac{1}{4}$yd (23cm) or 1FQ
SC 16: $\frac{1}{8}$yd (15cm) or 1FQ
SC 17: $\frac{1}{8}$yd (15cm) or 1FQ
SC 18: $\frac{1}{8}$yd (15cm) or 1FQ
SC 23: $\frac{1}{8}$yd (15cm) or 1FQ
PR 04: $\frac{1}{8}$yd (15cm) or 1FQ
PS 08: $\frac{1}{4}$yd (23cm) or 1FQ
PS 13: $\frac{1}{8}$yd (15cm) or 1FQ
GP 02-J: $\frac{1}{4}$yd (23cm) or 1FQ
GP 07-J: $\frac{1}{8}$yd (15cm) or 1FQ
GP 08-J: $\frac{1}{8}$yd (15cm) or 1FQ
BS 01: $\frac{1}{4}$yd (23cm) or 1FQ
NC 05: $\frac{1}{8}$yd (15cm) or 1FQ
AS 10: $\frac{1}{8}$yd (15cm) or 1FQ
Inner borders:
SC 04: See outer borders
Outer borders:
SC 04: $1\frac{1}{2}$yds (1.35m)
Backing:
NS 09: $2\frac{1}{4}$yds (2.05m)
Bias binding:
SC 04: See outer borders
Batting:
54in x 62in (137cm x 158cm)
Quilting thread:
Toning blue and light brown machine quilting thread

Foundation blocks

cut 3
Chinese coin
foundation papers
$8\frac{1}{2}$ in x $40\frac{1}{2}$ in
(21.5cm x 103cm)

cut 10
log cabin
foundation papers
$8\frac{1}{2}$ in x $8\frac{1}{2}$ in
(21.5cm x 21.5cm)

FOUNDATION PAPERS
The quilt centre is made up of 2 different foundation blocks, a Chinese Coin block and a Log Cabin block. Cut 3 Chinese Coin papers $8\frac{1}{2}$in x $40\frac{1}{2}$in (21.5cm x 103cm) and 10 Log Cabin papers $8\frac{1}{2}$in x $8\frac{1}{2}$in (21.5cm x 21.5cm) (see page 95). If you are not happy working the Log Cabin blocks totally free-hand, you will find 4 foundation papers printed at the back of this book (see pages 91 and 92). To use them, scale them up 200 percent on a photocopier and copy them until you have 10 papers of various designs. Check they measure the correct size before starting to stitch through them.

CUTTING OUT
Foundation patches:
Cut all patchwork fabrics into rough strips across the width of the fabric - see page 95 (cutting free-hand blocks).
Inner borders:
Cut 4 inner border strips $2\frac{1}{2}$in x $40\frac{1}{2}$in (6.5cm x 103cm) in SC 04.

Outer borders:
Cut 4 outer border strips $4\frac{1}{2}$in x $48\frac{1}{2}$in (11.5cm x 123cm) in SC 04.
Backing:
Cut 1 piece 45in x 54in (114cm x 137cm), and 2 pieces 18in x $27\frac{1}{2}$in (46cm x 70cm) in NS 09.
Bias binding:
Cut 6yds (5.4m) of bias binding $2\frac{1}{4}$in (6cm) wide from SC 04.

MAKING THE FOUNDATION BLOCKS
Make up the 10 Log Cabin blocks and 3 Chinese Coin blocks using the foundation piecing method (see page 96).

ASSEMBLING THE LOG CABIN BLOCKS
Arrange the Log Cabin blocks in 2 rows of 5, making sure you mix the foundation block colours well. Using a $\frac{1}{4}$in (6mm) seam allowance, join the blocks together to form 2 separate rows.

ASSEMBLING THE ROWS
Using the quilt assembly diagram as a guide, arrange the 3 Chinese Coin blocks alternating with the 2 Log Cabin rows. Place an inner border strip between each row of Chinese coins and Log Cabin. Using a $\frac{1}{4}$in (6mm) seam allowance, join the rows and borders together to form the quilt centre.

MAKING THE OUTER BORDERS
Using a $\frac{1}{4}$in (6mm) seam allowance, join the outer borders to the quilt edges following the numbered guide on the quilt assembly diagram.

Quilt assembly

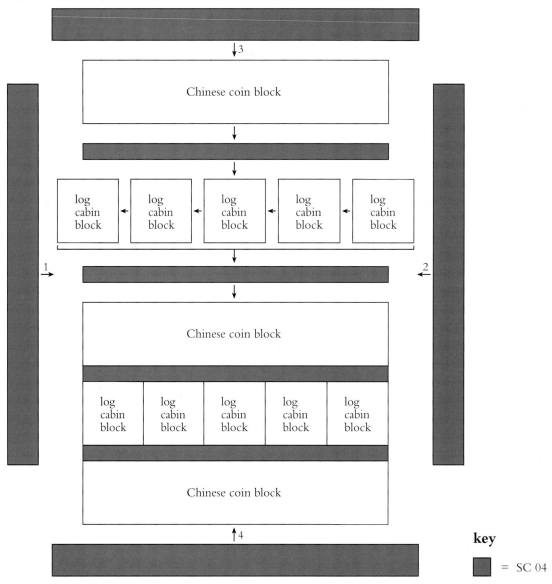

key

■ = SC 04

FINISHING THE QUILT

Press the assembled quilt top. Seam the 3 backing pieces together with a ⅜in (1cm) seam allowance to form one piece approximately 54in x 62in (137cm x 158cm). Layer the quilt top, batting and backing, and baste together (see page 98). Using the blue thread, spiral quilt in a very free-hand manner around each Log Cabin block - see quilting diagram (a). Using the quilting diagram (b) as a guide, free-motion quilt in 1 long wavy line up each Chinese Coin block, roughly following the fabric strips. Using the light brown thread, free-motion quilt the borders in a very random fashion. Trim the quilt edges and attach the binding (see page 99).

Quilting log cabin blocks

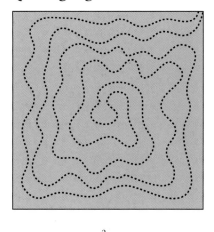

a

Quilting Chinese coin blocks

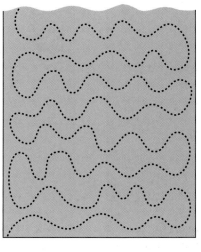

b

Moroccan Door

KAFFE FASSETT

Inspiration for this project came from a massive wooden door, which Kaffe saw on a visit to Marrakech. It had been painted red and white and the panels formed a wonderful geometric design. Based on the traditional Log Cabin design, this quilt needs to be worked very precisely and to make handling easier, we feel foundation piecing is best method for this quilt.

SIZE OF QUILT
The finished quilt will measure approximately 40in x 60in (101.5cm x 152.5cm).

MATERIALS
Patchwork fabrics:
SC 07: ½yd (45cm)
SC 10: ⅔yd (60cm)
SC 28: see backing
GP 01-R: ⅓yd (30cm)
GP 07-J: ¼yd (23cm)
Backing:
SC 28: 3yds (2.7m)
Pieced binding:
See patchwork fabrics

Foundation blocks

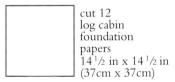

cut 12
log cabin
foundation
papers
14½ in x 14½ in
(37cm x 37cm)

FOUNDATION PAPERS
The centre is made of 12 Log Cabin blocks worked on foundation papers, 5 of which are cut diagonally in half to form the outer triangles. Cut 12 foundation papers 14½in x 14½in (37cm x 37cm). See page 95.

CUTTING OUT
Foundation strips:
Using a rotary cutter, very accurately cut 1½in- (4cm-) wide strips across width of 45in- (114cm-) wide fabric. Cut 4 in GP 07-J, 5 in GP 01-R, 10 in SC 07, 11 in SC 10 and 28 in SC 28.

Backing:
Cut 1 piece 45in x 61in (114cm x 155cm) in SC 28.
Pieced binding:
Cut remainder of dark fabrics into 2¼in- (6cm-) wide strips across width of fabric, and cut into pieces 4 - 6in (10 -15cm) long. Using a ¼in (6mm) seam allowance, join the pieces end to end, alternating the colours to form 5⅔yd (5.7m) of straight cut binding.

MAKING THE FOUNDATION BLOCKS
Following key and Wall hanging assembly diagrams in strict order, make up 12 precise Log Cabin foundation blocks (see page 96). Draw a diagonal line across right side of blocks H, I, J, K and L and work a line of machine stay stitches ¼in (6mm), each side of the line. Cut the blocks in half along the drawn line.

Wall hanging assembly and block combinations

½ of block J   ½ of block I

½ of block H

½ of block I

½ of block K

block A

½ of block L

block B

block C

½ of block K

block D

½ of block L

block E

block F

½ of block H

block G

½ of block I   ½ of block J

key   ■ = GP 01-R   ■ = GP 07-J   ■ = SC 07   ■ = SC 10   ■ = SC 28

ASSEMBLING THE BLOCKS

Arrange the full and half foundation blocks in 5 rows as shown in the wall hanging assembly diagram.

Using a ¼in (6mm) seam allowance join the blocks together into rows and then join the rows to form the patchwork top.

FINISHING THE HANGING

Press the assembled patchwork top and layer the top and backing.

Baste together (see page 98).

Trim the wall hanging edges and attach the binding (see page 99).

Turn to page 101 in the Patchwork know-how section, for instructions on how to prepare a patchwork for hanging.

Some Like It Hot

KIM HARGREAVES

This fabulous large quilt is designed to drape on the floor. Because it involves handling large panels of fabric we have given it two stars, and like making a large set of curtains, you will need space for cutting out and working. To help the panels fit together well it is best to pin them first at right-angles to the seam, before stitching.

SIZE OF QUILT

The finished quilt will measure approximately 109in x 109in (270cm x 270cm).

MATERIALS

Fabrics:
SC 02: 3yds (2.7m)
SC 07: 5²⁄₃yds (5.1m)
Backing:
SC 25: 10¹⁄₄yds (9.25m)
Straight cut binding:
SC 25: see backing
Batting:
114in x 114in (290cm x 290cm)
Quilting thread:
Matching hand quilting thread

CUTTING OUT

Central panels:
Cut 2 bands 20¹⁄₂in x 100¹⁄₂in (51cm x 255cm) in SC 02 and 3 bands in SC07.
Borders:
Cut 2 side borders 4³⁄₄in x 100¹⁄₂in (12cm x 255cm) and 2 end borders 4³⁄₄in x 109in (12cm x 277cm) in SC 25.
Backing:
Cut 2 pieces 45in x 114in (114cm x 290cm) and 1 piece 26in x 114in (66cm x 290cm) in SC 25.
Straight cut binding:
Cut 10 strips 2¹⁄₂in- (6.5cm-) wide x width of fabric in SC 25, to form 12¹⁄₂yds (11.25m) of binding.

ASSEMBLING THE QUILT CENTRE

Using a ¹⁄₄in (6mm) seam allowance, join the central panels together, alternating the colours.

ATTACHING THE BORDERS

Using a ¹⁄₄in (6mm) seam allowance, attach the 2 side borders and then the end borders to the quilt edges.

FINISHING THE QUILT

Press the assembled quilt top. Seam the 3 fabric backing pieces together with a ³⁄₈in (1cm) seam allowance to form one very piece approximately 114in x 114in (290cm x 290cm).

Layer the quilt top, batting and backing, and baste together (see page 98).

Work 19 rows of hand quilting stitches in a chevron pattern along each panel. To do this, measure up along the seam lines and to outer edges of the quilt at 5in (12.5cm) intervals, and also mark up the centre of each panel at intervals of 5in (12.5cm). Use pins to mark positions. Join pins with either pieces of Quilters' tape or a temporary fabric marker (see quilting diagram below), and use lines as a stitch guide.

Trim the quilt edges and attach the binding (see page 99).

Panel quilting

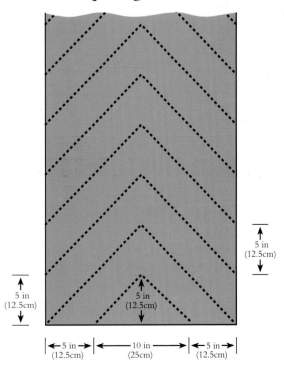

Saffron Tray Cloth

KIM HARGREAVES

Following on the theme of Some Like It Hot, Kim has designed this great tray cloth with appliquéd square patches - it has real Zen appeal. But, don't just think of it as a tray cloth - if you made six or eight of them, they would become a very stylish addition to any table as placemats

SIZE OF TRAY CLOTH

The finished tray cloth will measure approximately 9¼in x 15¼in (23.5cm x 39cm).

MATERIALS

Appliqué and backing fabric:
SC 02: ⅓yd (30cm) or 1FQ
Top fabric:
SC 01: ⅓yd (30cm) or 1FQ
Lightweight iron-on interfacing:
⅓yd (30cm) x 35½in (90cm) wide
Paper-backed adhesive web:
⅛yd (15cm) ox35½in (90cm) wide
Appliqué thread:
Matching machine threads

PATCH SHAPES

The appliqué on this cloth is formed from a 1½in (4cm) square.

CUTTING OUT

Top and backing:
Cut a rectangle 10in x 16in (25.5cm x 40.5cm) in SC 01 for the top and one in SC 02 for the backing.

Appliqué squares:
Iron the adhesive web on to the reverse side of the remaining fabric SC 02, and cut 8 x 1½in (4cm) squares.

APPLIQUÉING THE TRAY CLOTH

Iron interfacing to the reverse side of the top piece, and arrange the squares on to the right side of the top in a single row. Machine appliqué them in position (see page 97).

FINISHING THE TRAY CLOTH

Lay backing onto right side of top and stitch together around all sides, leaving an opening along one side. Clip corners and turn to right side. Press seamed edges flat and slip stitch opening edges together.

THE KAFFE FASSETT FABRIC COLLECTION

100% Cotton

Fabric width 45ins (114cm)

Shot Cotton

SC01 SC02 SC03 SC04 SC05 SC06

SC07 SC08 SC09 SC10 SC11 SC12

SC13 SC14 SC15 SC16 SC17 SC18

SC19 SC20 SC21 SC22 SC23 SC24

SC25 SC26 SC27 SC28 SC29 SC30

SC31 SC32 SC33 SC34 SC35 SC36

Roman Stripe

RS01 RS02 RS03 RS04 RS05 RS06

RS07 RS08

Ombre Stripe

OS01 OS02 OS04 OS05

Blue & White Stripe   **Alternate**

BWS01 BWS02   AS01 AS03 AS10 AS21

Pachrangi

PS01 PS04 PS05 PS08 PS13 PS15

Broad Stripe

PS22 BS01 BS06 BS08 BS11 BS23

Narrow Stripe

NS01 NS08 NS09 NS13 NS16 NS17

The story behind Kaffe's Patchwork fabric range is an interesting one. Each year he gives some time to assist artisans around the world, and the stripes, checks and plains in this range are all individully woven on simple hand looms, through the Fair Trading Trusts in India. Being hand-woven, this means that no two fabrics are identical, and the small imperfections that occur in the process all add to the inherent beauty of these cloths. This makes for some very exciting design possibilities, whether you're following our suggested colour recipes, or working out your own.

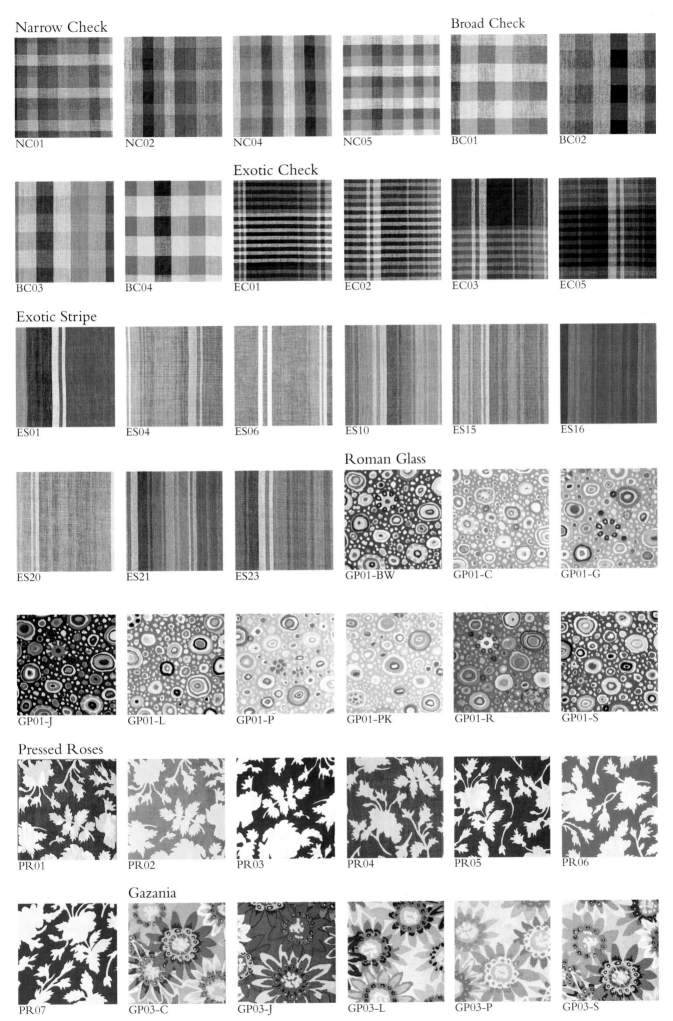

Narrow Check

NC01 NC02 NC04 NC05

Broad Check

BC01 BC02

BC03 BC04

Exotic Check

EC01 EC02 EC03 EC05

Exotic Stripe

ES01 ES04 ES06 ES10 ES15 ES16

ES20 ES21 ES23

Roman Glass

GP01-BW GP01-C GP01-G

GP01-J GP01-L GP01-P GP01-PK GP01-R GP01-S

Pressed Roses

PR01 PR02 PR03 PR04 PR05 PR06

Gazania

PR07 GP03-C GP03-J GP03-L GP03-P GP03-S

75

Damask

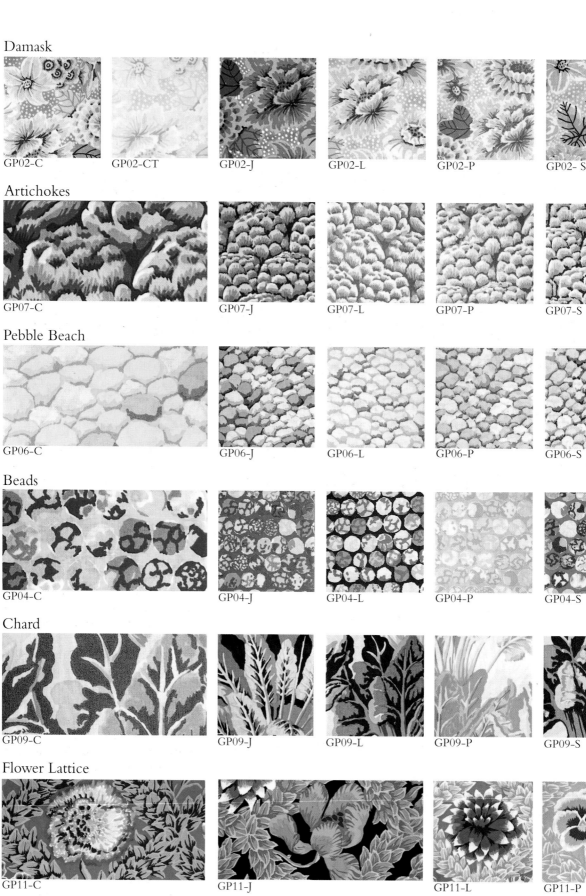

GP02-C   GP02-CT   GP02-J   GP02-L   GP02-P   GP02-S

Artichokes

GP07-C   GP07-J   GP07-L   GP07-P   GP07-S

Pebble Beach

GP06-C   GP06-J   GP06-L   GP06-P   GP06-S

Beads

GP04-C   GP04-J   GP04-L   GP04-P   GP04-S

Chard

GP09-C   GP09-J   GP09-L   GP09-P   GP09-S

Flower Lattice

GP11-C   GP11-J   GP11-L   GP11-P

Forget-me-not Rose

GP11-S   GP11-SU   GP08-C   GP08-J   GP08-L   GP08-S

An Amish Fascination

Roberta Horton is an internationally acclaimed quiltmaker, designer, author and teacher. Here she talks about the influence that Amish design and colour has had on her work. For this book Roberta has designed Indiana Baskets design using a selection of fabrics from the Rowan Kaffe Fassett fabric collection.

"Listen to the fabric – it tells you how to behave". Admired for her handling of colour and combinations of textiles, Roberta Horton has always loved fabrics, however small the scraps. From an early age she used them to dress her dolls and learned to sew to make the clothes. She credits her Scottish/Irish grandmother with passing on an artistic streak, and believes her Russian and Hungarian ancestors also provided her with subconscious inspiration.

Roberta's early interest in fabrics led her to studying textiles at the University of California at Berkeley. She started her

Left: Nine Patch from *An Amish Adventure*

working life as a Home Economics teacher, but it wasn't long before her real passion pulled her away to a different path. Her second career revolves entirely around quilts - teaching, lecturing, writing, making and continually discovering more about them. Roberta loves to delve into the history, studying antique quilts and learning about the people who made them. This has lead to a fascination with the Amish people – both their lifestyle and their quilts - and the Amish simplicity of design and approach to colour have strongly influenced her own style.

"Since I encountered my first Amish quilt more than twenty years ago I have been completely fascinated. I have travelled thousands of miles to attend shows featuring them and continue to read everything I can about the Amish people and their lifestyle. And this is a love affair that doesn't end as I've been fortunate enough to share this fascination with other quilters in Japan, New Zealand, South Africa and in Europe", says Roberta.

In her book *An Amish Adventure*, Roberta Horton talks about the founding of the Amish movement. In the mid-16th century in Switzerland a religious group separated from the main church. They became known as the Mennonites and were persecuted for their beliefs. A splinter group under the leadership of Jacob Ammann eventually emerged as the Amish. These people began to emigrate

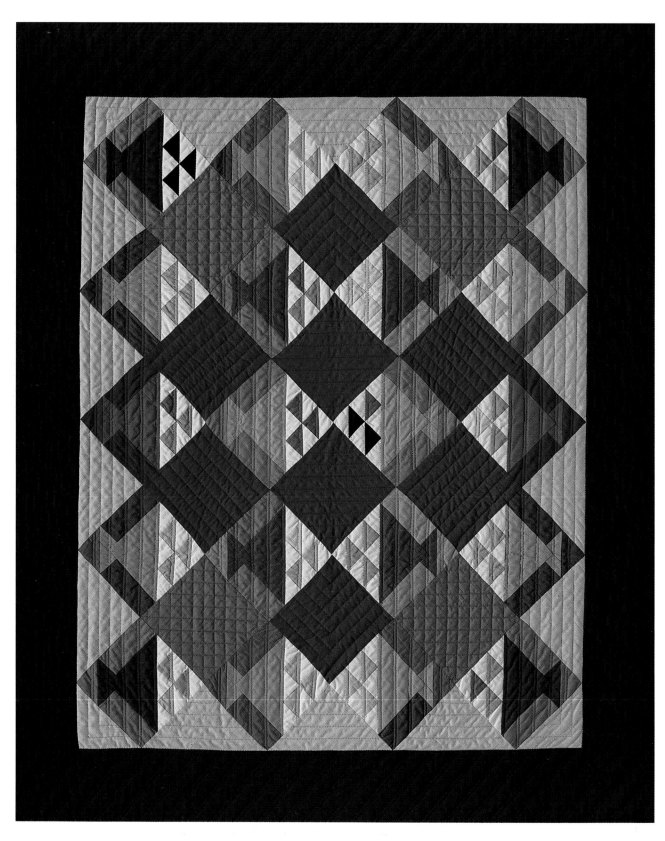

to America in the 1730s, and since that time they have lived in the U.S. in rural farming communities in groups of limited numbers. They are self-governed, maintaining their distance from the outside world by being as self-sufficient as possible. Although they pay taxes, they build and support their own schools and do not collect any state benefits, nor do they vote or undertake military service. Simplicity in all things remains central to their lives, which still revolve around their religion. The farms use no modern technology and work is deemed to be an important part of every stage of life.

She points out that Amish families are patriarchal, and the women primarily concerned with bringing up children. Many

Opposite: Indiana Baskets (original version); above left: Ocean Waves, both from *An Amish Adventure*; above right: Frau Horton from *Scrap Quilts*

love to quilt, but sewing is undertaken mainly for practical reasons. Quilts are made firstly for warmth and new ones are made to replace worn out ones, as well as at times of birth and marriage. Today many Amish women also make quilts to sell to the outside world. Quiltmaking in Amish communities is often a family affair with all generations taking part, the children helping with cutting the pieces. The tradition of mutual assistance remains strong.

Amish washday, with the clothes hanging on the line provides a snapshot of the colour palette they use for their quilts and offers a clue to their design approach. The original colours of the Pennsylvanian Amish palette are limited to black and the part of the colour wheel that leads from green, via blue, to red, leaving out oranges, yellows, and yellow-green shades. Their clothes are simple and fairly uniform in style. The quilt designs, too, are simple but distinctive, directly reflecting the lifestyle and philosophy of the people.

In her continuing research, Roberta was surprised to find the variety of colours used and the range of colour values – from dark to palest pastel – that might be used in one quilt. In another only bright, pure colours have been selected, or only greyed-out, mysterious tones. "No-one knows why the Amish choose to use colour as they do, but the end result is very strong and powerful. Perhaps that is reason enough – you will find your own work changed after working with Amish colours", she says.

Roberta has also learned to combine clear colours with greyed shades, either as a 'sparkle' (a pale clear colour plus a dark one) or a 'glow' (a medium bright, clear colour plus a dark one). These are her own words that she uses to put across her teaching. Most Amish women work with whatever is to hand, rather than seeking out a particular colour or tone. "The first thing I learned [from the Amish] was the power of mismatching. Generally quilters work with colours that are based on lessons learned from wearing clothing, with the preference being for a dyed-to-match look. The Amish make do, and substitute something close to the original when they run out of a fabric. This gives energy to the quilt." They work with solid colours, regarding printed fabrics as too worldly. The designs are not laid down but are passed on from mother to daughter. Some women repeat the same pattern, but using different fabrics, while others draft new ones, but always retaining the distinctive style. Following a visit to the Amish community in Lancaster Country, Pennsylvania in 1980, Roberta initiated a series of six-week quilting classes which have remained popular ever since. She is now in demand around the world for these classes and for lectures on the subject. Her philosophy starts with an exhortation to "suspend your self doubts and do as I say – forget the word 'can't' and try a few exercises. You really must do them; reading is not enough."

Roberta has been teaching about Amish patchwork and quilting for over twenty years and still enjoys giving a class. "Even in my six and twelve hour versions the participants tell me how much they have learned about colour, using it in combinations they haven't tried before. Through studying a tradition we come full circle back to the beginning, richer for the experience".

A BRIEF INTRODUCTION TO AMISH PATCHING, FROM ROBERTA:
Start with a good selection of solid colour fabrics, including several shades of black. Experiment with a straightforward design such as a standard nine-patch quilt. This is complex enough to represent an enjoyable challenge and also offers an opportunity to discover something of the Amish approach to colour interaction, asymmetrical placement and bordering.

Background and Patches

1. Select three background colours. They should be light to medium shades of one colour or three very similar colours of the same value, or tone. Remember – aim to mismatch to create an Amish feel.

2. Two more colours will be required for the nine-patches. One should be darker than anything you have selected for the background. The other should be of a medium to light value, but not too similar in colour to the three background fabrics chosen. If the first nine-patch combination blends too much with the background, try another combination. This is known as 'auditioning'.

3. Make sixteen, nine-patch blocks from the last two fabrics selected. Most will have five dark pieces and four medium or light pieces. Several of your blocks should combine four dark and five light pieces. Don't be tempted to go for half of each combination - be Amish, not English!

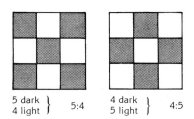

5 dark } 5:4   4 dark } 4:5
4 light   5 light

4. Now test the different placements of the background squares, using the three colours originally selected. Experiment with any or all of six possible combinations. Decisions can now be taken regarding the perimeter triangles. Notice how

some of the colours may feel lighter or darker as their positions are moved around. The value of the colour is how light or dark it is. This is always relative – it depends on what else is being used around it and in the project.

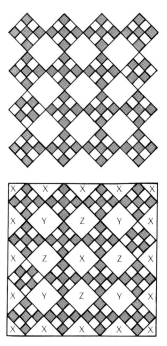

X = colour in centre, also perimeter triangles
Y = colour in corner blocks
Z = colour in middle blocks

Borders

Amish quilts are well-known for their wide borders of single colours or pieces, but can also have a narrow inner border between this and the central design. Corner blocks are also used in the inner and/or outer borders. These corners are unmitred – again, the simple approach.

5. Select inner, outer and corner blocks from the five fabrics already used in the project and apply the auditioning process. Once again, experimentation is the key. Don't be afraid to try everything, even colours that you don't think will work. You may be in for a surprise.

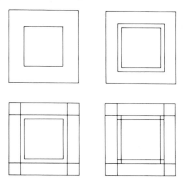

An Amish Adventure by Roberta Horton is published by C & T Publishing in the USA and is distributed in the UK through Windsor Books. Call 01865 361122 for stockist details.

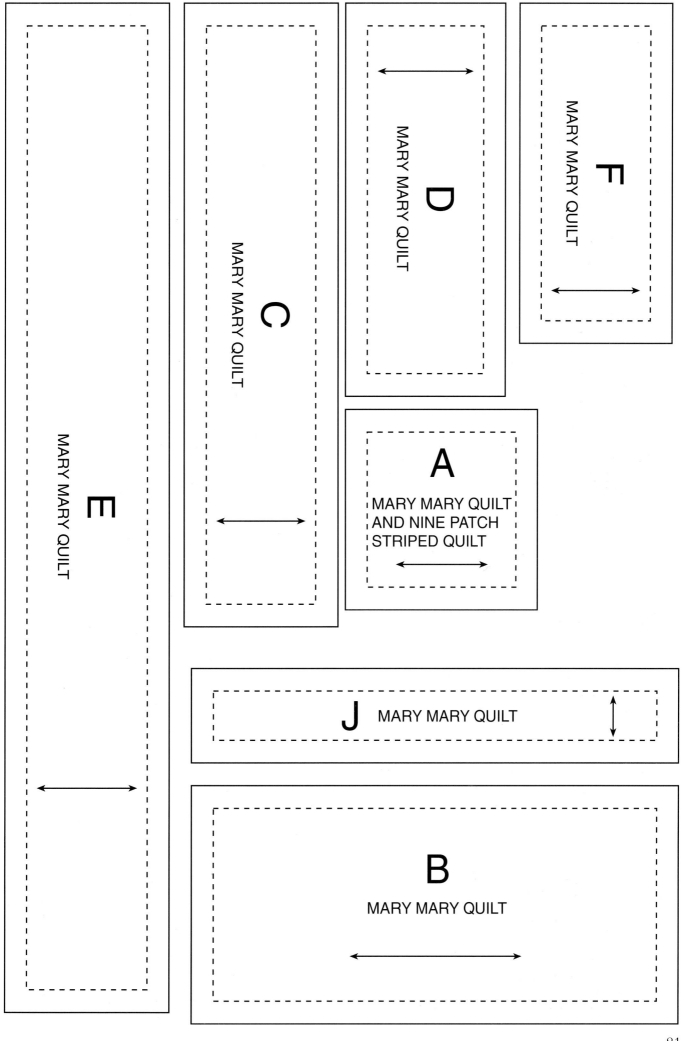

E

MARY MARY QUILT

C

MARY MARY QUILT

D

MARY MARY QUILT

F

MARY MARY QUILT

A

MARY MARY QUILT
AND NINE PATCH
STRIPED QUILT

J   MARY MARY QUILT

B

MARY MARY QUILT

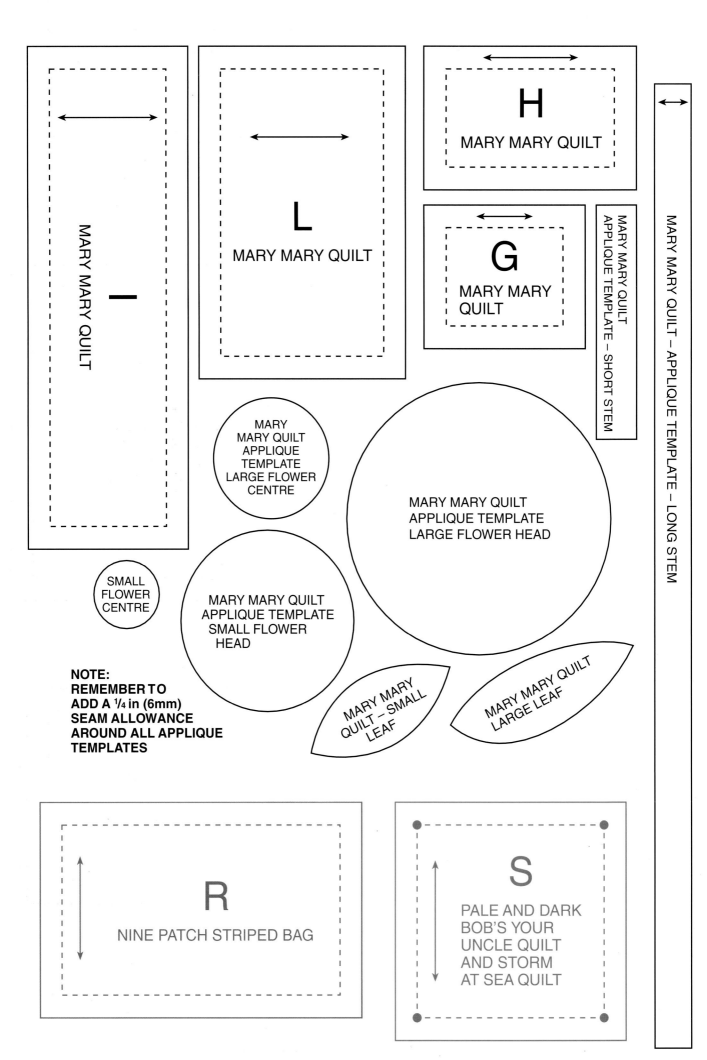

MARY MARY QUILT

L
MARY MARY QUILT

H
MARY MARY QUILT

G
MARY MARY QUILT

I
MARY MARY QUILT

MARY MARY QUILT APPLIQUE TEMPLATE – SHORT STEM

MARY MARY QUILT – APPLIQUE TEMPLATE – LONG STEM

MARY MARY QUILT APPLIQUE TEMPLATE LARGE FLOWER CENTRE

SMALL FLOWER CENTRE

MARY MARY QUILT APPLIQUE TEMPLATE SMALL FLOWER HEAD

MARY MARY QUILT APPLIQUE TEMPLATE LARGE FLOWER HEAD

MARY MARY QUILT – SMALL LEAF

MARY MARY QUILT LARGE LEAF

**NOTE:
REMEMBER TO
ADD A ¼ in (6mm)
SEAM ALLOWANCE
AROUND ALL APPLIQUE
TEMPLATES**

R
NINE PATCH STRIPED BAG

S
PALE AND DARK
BOB'S YOUR
UNCLE QUILT
AND STORM
AT SEA QUILT

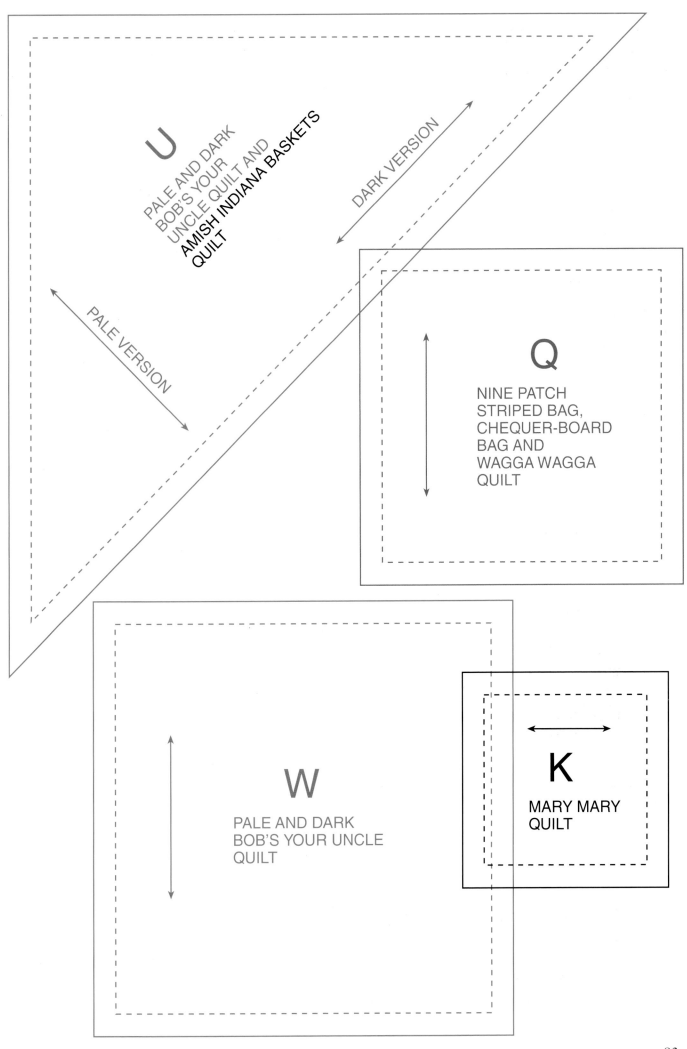

U

PALE AND DARK
BOB'S YOUR
UNCLE QUILT AND
AMISH INDIANA BASKETS
QUILT

DARK VERSION

PALE VERSION

Q

NINE PATCH
STRIPED BAG,
CHEQUER-BOARD
BAG AND
WAGGA WAGGA
QUILT

W

PALE AND DARK
BOB'S YOUR UNCLE
QUILT

K

MARY MARY
QUILT

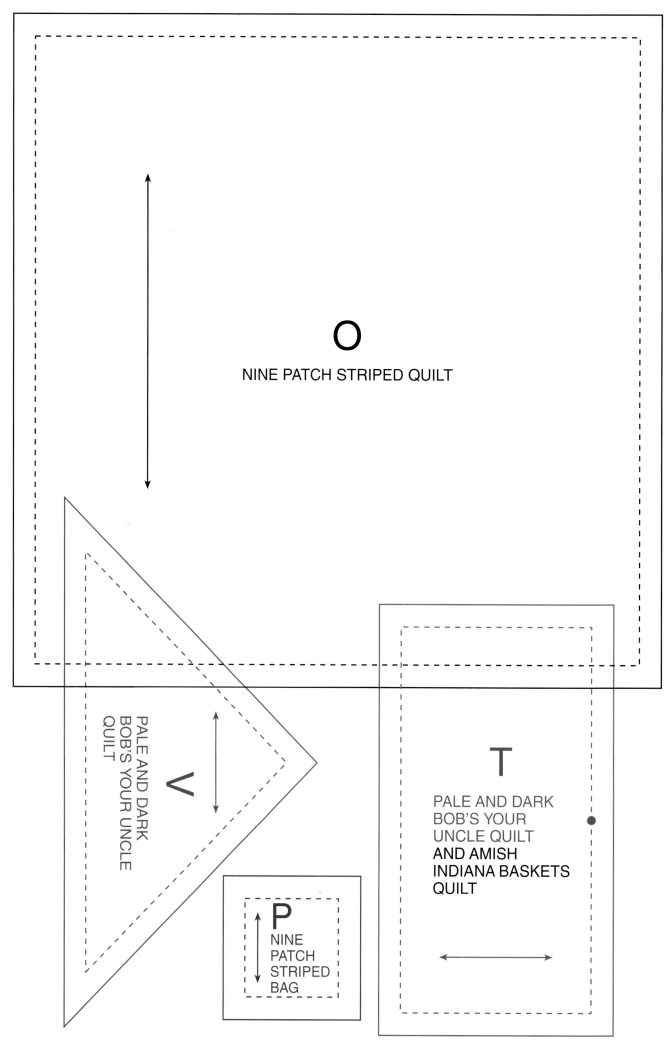

O

NINE PATCH STRIPED QUILT

V

PALE AND DARK
BOB'S YOUR UNCLE
QUILT

P

NINE
PATCH
STRIPED
BAG

T

PALE AND DARK
BOB'S YOUR
UNCLE QUILT
AND AMISH
INDIANA BASKETS
QUILT

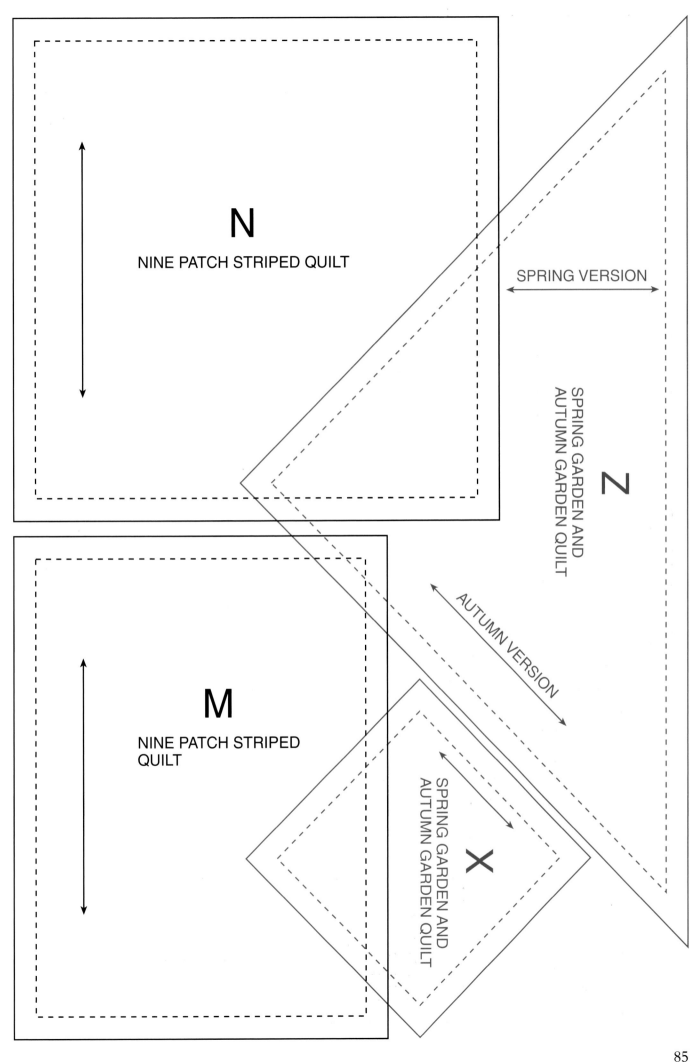

N

NINE PATCH STRIPED QUILT

SPRING VERSION

SPRING GARDEN AND
AUTUMN GARDEN QUILT

Z

AUTUMN VERSION

M

NINE PATCH STRIPED
QUILT

SPRING GARDEN AND
AUTUMN GARDEN QUILT

X

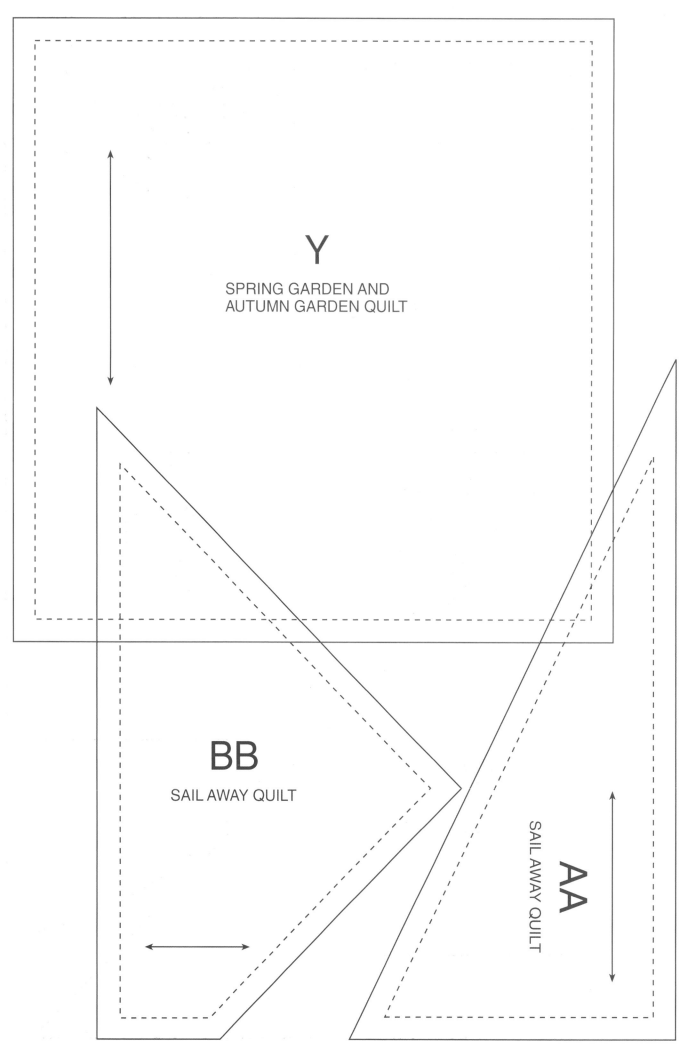

Y

SPRING GARDEN AND
AUTUMN GARDEN QUILT

BB

SAIL AWAY QUILT

AA

SAIL AWAY QUILT

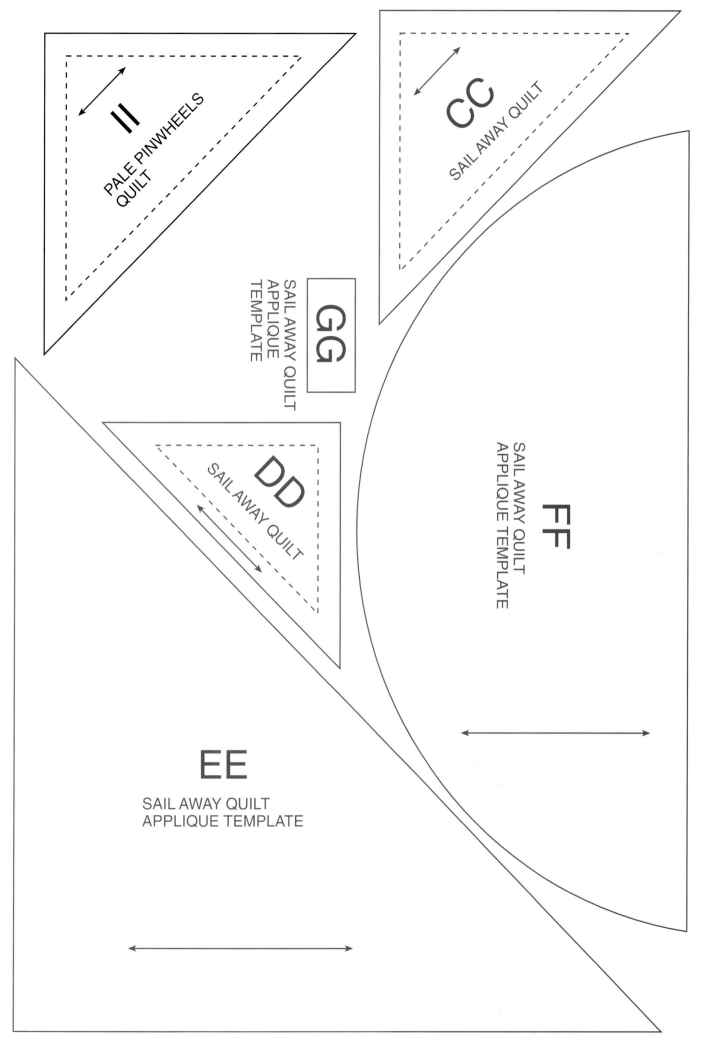

II
PALE PINWHEELS
QUILT

CC
SAIL AWAY QUILT

GG
SAIL AWAY QUILT
APPLIQUE
TEMPLATE

DD
SAIL AWAY QUILT

FF
SAIL AWAY QUILT
APPLIQUE TEMPLATE

EE
SAIL AWAY QUILT
APPLIQUE TEMPLATE

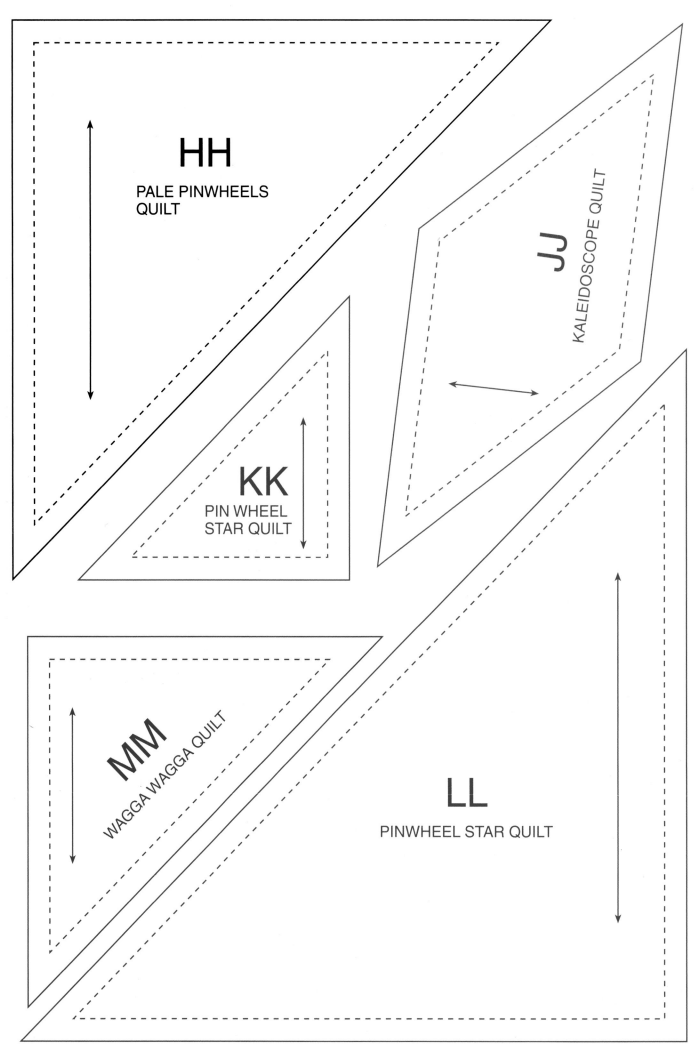

HH
PALE PINWHEELS
QUILT

JJ
KALEIDOSCOPE QUILT

KK
PIN WHEEL
STAR QUILT

MM
WAGGA WAGGA QUILT

LL
PINWHEEL STAR QUILT

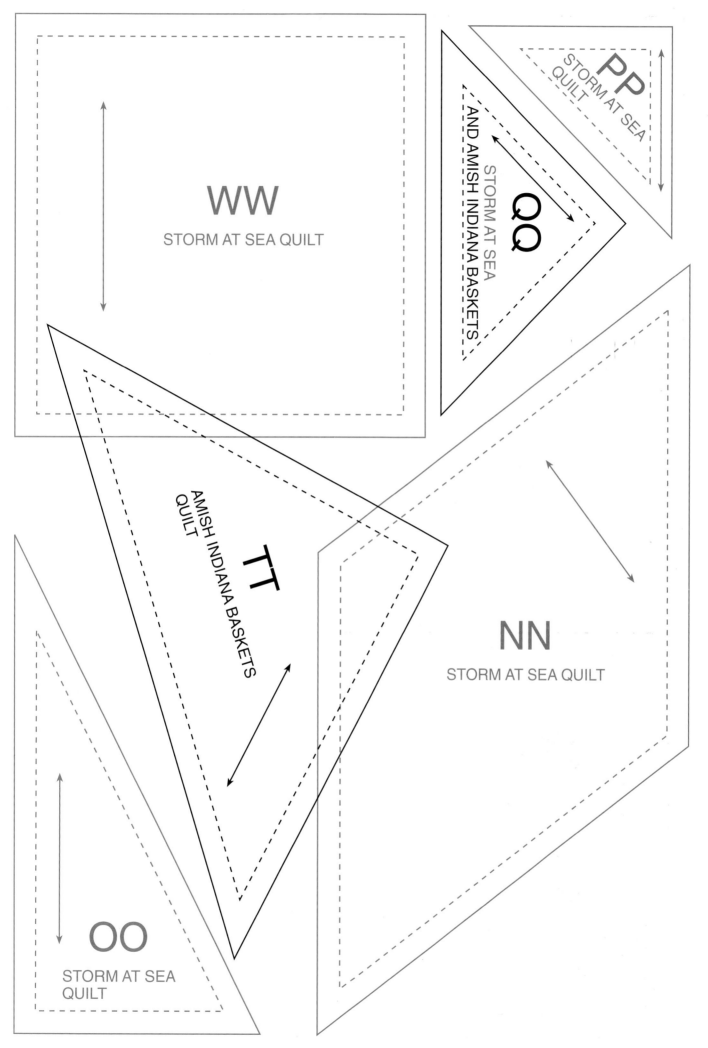

WW
STORM AT SEA QUILT

PP
STORM AT SEA
QUILT

QQ
STORM AT SEA
AND AMISH INDIANA BASKETS

TT
AMISH INDIANA BASKETS
QUILT

NN
STORM AT SEA QUILT

OO
STORM AT SEA
QUILT

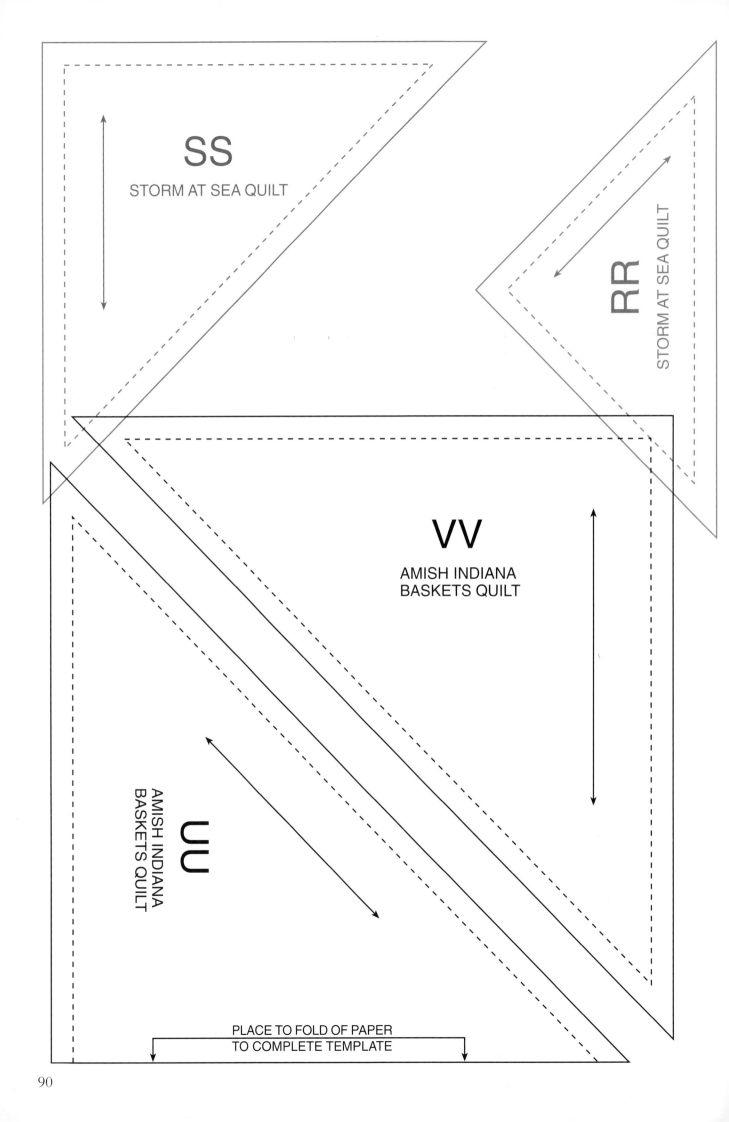

SS
STORM AT SEA QUILT

RR
STORM AT SEA QUILT

VV
AMISH INDIANA
BASKETS QUILT

UU
AMISH INDIANA
BASKETS QUILT

PLACE TO FOLD OF PAPER
TO COMPLETE TEMPLATE

CHINESE COINS AND LOG CABIN QUILT

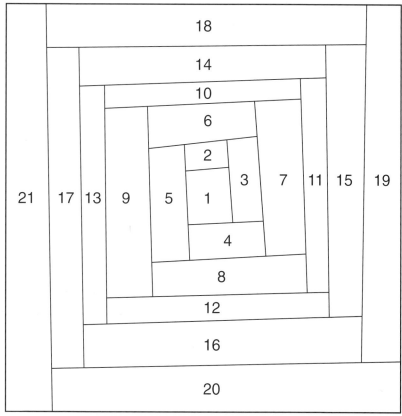

THESE FOUNDATION BLOCKS ARE PRINTED AT 50% THEIR CORRECT SIZE.

TO USE, SCALE THEM UP 200% ON A PHOTOCOPIER TO MEASURE 8½ in x 8½ in (21.5cm x 21.5cm).

LOG CABIN FOUNDATION BLOCK 1

CHINESE COINS AND LOG CABIN QUILT

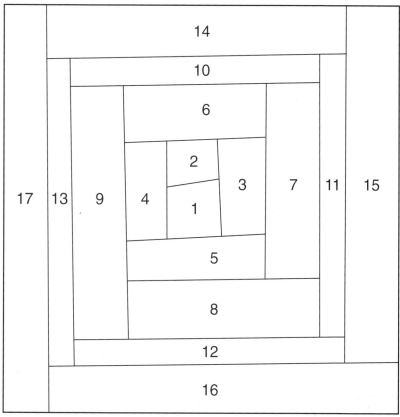

LOG CABIN FOUNDATION BLOCK 2

CHINESE COINS AND LOG CABIN QUILT

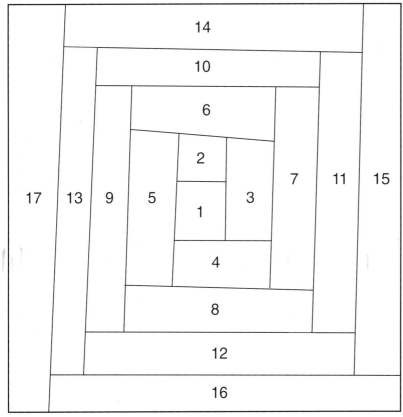

THESE FOUNDATION BLOCKS ARE PRINTED AT 50% THEIR CORRECT SIZE.

TO USE, SCALE THEM UP 200% ON A PHOTOCOPIER TO MEASURE 8½ in x 8½ in (21.5cm x 21.5cm).

LOG CABIN FOUNDATION BLOCK 3

CHINESE COINS AND LOG CABIN QUILT

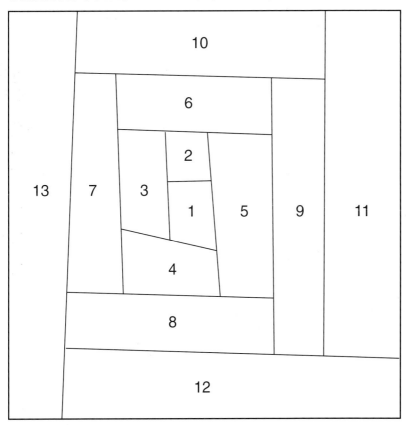

LOG CABIN FOUNDATION BLOCK 4

JUPITER SUNSET WALL HANGING
FOUNDATION BLOCK EXAMPLE

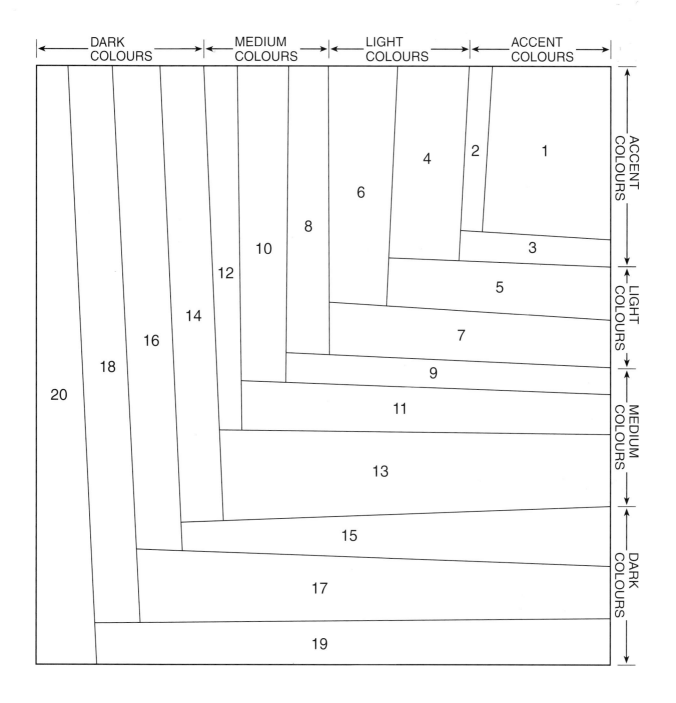

THIS FOUNDATION BLOCK IS
PRINTED AT 50% ITS CORRECT
SIZE.

TO USE, SCALE IT UP 200% ON
A PHOTOCOPIER TO MEASURE
12½ in x 12½ in (32cm x 32cm).

PATCHWORK KNOW-HOW

These instructions are intended for the novice quilt maker and do not cover all techniques used in making patchwork and patchwork quilts. They provide the basic information needed to make the projects in this book, along with some useful tips. Try not to become overwhelmed by technique - patchwork is a craft which should be enjoyed.

Preparing the fabric

Prewash all new fabrics before you begin, to ensure that there will be no uneven shrinkage and no bleeding of colours when the quilt is laundered. Press the fabric whilst it is still damp to return crispness to it.

Making templates

Templates are the best made from transparent template plastic, which is not only durable, but allows you to see the fabric and select certain motifs. You can also make them from thin stiff cardboard if template plastic is not available. If you choose cardboard, paint the edges of the finished template with nail polish to give it longer life.

Templates for machine-piecing

1 Trace off the actual-sized template provided either directly on to template plastic, or tracing paper, and then on to thin cardboard. Use a ruler to help you trace off the straight cutting line, dotted seam line and grainlines.
Some of the templates in this book are so large that we have only been able to give you half of them. Before transferring them on to plastic or card, trace off the half template, place the fold edge up to the fold of a piece of paper, and carefully draw around the shape. Cut out the paper double thickness, and open out for the completed template.

2 Cut out the traced off template using a craft knife, ruler and a self-healing cutting mat (see page 101 for definition).

3 Punch holes in the corners of the template, at each point on the seam line, using a hole punch.

Templates for hand-piecing

• Make a template as shown above, but do not trace off the cutting line. Use the dotted seam line as the outer edge of the template.

• This template allows you to draw the seam lines directly on to the fabric. The seam allowances can then be cut by eye around the patch.

Cutting the fabric

On the individual instructions for each patchwork, you will find a summary of all the patch shapes used.
Always mark and cut out any border and binding strips first, followed by the largest patch shapes and finally the smallest ones, to make the most efficient use of your fabric. The border and binding strips are best cut using a rotary cutter.

Rotary cutting

Rotary cut strips are often cut across the fabric from selvedge to selvedge. With the projects we do, be certain to cut the strips running the desired direction.

1 Before beginning to cut, press out any folds or creases in the fabric. If you are cutting a large piece of fabric, you will need to fold it several times to fit the cutting mat. When there is only a single fold, place the fold facing you. If the fabric is too wide to be folded only once, fold it concertina-style until it fits your mat. A small rotary cutter with a sharp blade will cut up to 6 layers of fabric; a large cutter up to 8 layers.

2 To ensure that your cut strips are straight and even, the folds must be placed exactly parallel to the straight edges of the fabric and along a line on the cutting mat.

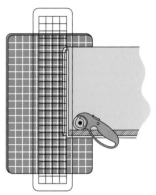

3 Place a plastic ruler over the raw edge of the fabric, overlapping it about $\frac{1}{2}$in (1.25cm). Make sure that the ruler is at right angles to both the straight edges and the fold to ensure that you cut along the straight grain. Press down on the ruler and wheel the cutter away from yourself along the edge of the ruler.

4 Open out the fabric to check the edge. Don't worry if it's not perfectly straight; a little wiggle will not show when the quilt is stitched together. Re-fold fabric as shown in step 1, then place the ruler over the trimmed edge, aligning edge with the markings on the ruler that match the correct strip width. Cut strip along the edge of the ruler.

Using templates

The most efficient way to cut out templates is by first rotary cutting a strip of fabric the width stated for your template, and then marking off your templates along the strip, edge to edge at the required angle. This method leaves hardly any waste and gives a random effect to your patches.
A less efficient method is to fussy cut, where the templates are cut individually by placing them on particular motifs or stripes, to create special effects. Although this method is more wasteful it yields very interesting results.

1 Place the template face down on the wrong side of the fabric, with the grain line arrow following the straight grain of the fabric, if indicated. Be careful though - check with your individual instructions, as some instructions may ask you to cut patches on varying grains.

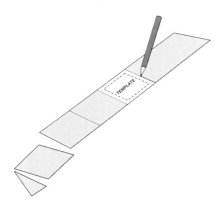

2 Hold the template firmly in place and draw around it with a sharp pencil or crayon, marking in the corner dots or seam lines. To save fabric, position patches close together or even touching. Don't worry if outlines positioned on the straight grain when drawn on striped fabrics do not always match the stripes when cut - this will add a degree of visual excitement to the patchwork!

3 Once you've drawn all the pieces needed, you are ready to cut the fabric, with either a rotary cutter and ruler, or a pair of sharp sewing scissors.

Foundation piecing

In foundation piecing, the patchwork design is worked onto paper patterns the exact size of each finished block, including seam allowances. During the stitching process, the patches are joined together by sewing through the foundation pattern to form the finished block.

Preparing foundation block patterns

1 Cut the correct number of foundation blocks for your quilt, from either newsprint (preferably un-printed), greaseproof paper, or alternatively use one of the new non-woven tear-away backings. These should be cut to the stated size on your project (the finished size of the block, plus a ¼in (6mm) seam allowance around all four sides).

2 If working a square Log Cabin design, draw two diagonal lines on each block from corner to corner, bisecting at the centre.

Cutting foundation patches

Some foundation projects in this book are worked very precisely and accurately, whilst others are meant to be worked free-hand in a very loose manner, creating a very different overall effect.

Each method needs to be treated differently when cutting out:

- For precise blocks, you will need to rotary cut your strips of fabric very accurately with a plastic ruler to the widths stated for your project.

- For free-hand blocks, cut the strips free-hand, without a ruler, so that you don't end up with perfect straight edges.
  Little wiggles enhance the effect. Make some of your strips wedge shaped and vary the strip widths. There will be no definite strip widths stated for your project - the choice is yours, so be as creative as you please.

Arranging cut patches

- Quilt instructions always give you a layout for how to arrange the various patch shapes to form the overall geometrical design. It is possible though to simply start stitching the cut patches together at random, but you will often create a much better effect if you plan the design first.

- To plan lay the patches out on the floor or stick them to a large flannel or felt-covered board, then stand back to study the effect. If you are not happy with the result, swap the patches around until you reach the desired effect.

Basic hand- and machine-piecing

Patches can be joined together by hand or machine.
Machine stitching is quicker, but hand assembly allows you to carry your patches around with you and work on them in every spare moment. The choice is yours. For techniques that are new to you, practise on scrap pieces of fabric until you feel confident.

Machine-piecing

Follow the quilt instructions for the order in which to piece the individual patchwork blocks and then assemble the blocks together in rows.

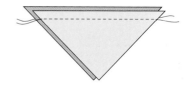

1 Seam lines are not marked on the fabric, so stitch ¼in (6mm) seams using the machine needle plate, a ¼in- (6mm-) wide machine foot, or tape stuck to the machine as a guide. Pin two patches with right sides together, matching edges. Set your machine at 10-12 stitches per inch (2.5cm) and stitch seams from edge to edge, removing pins as you feed the fabric through the machine.

2 Press the seams of each patchwork block to one side before attempting to join it to another block.

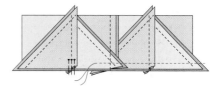

3 When joining rows of blocks, make sure that adjacent seam allowances are pressed in opposite directions to reduce bulk and make matching easier. Pin pieces together directly through the stitch line and to the right and left of the seam. Remove pins as you sew. Continue pressing seams to one side as you work.

Hand-piecing

1 Pin two patches with right sides together, so that the marked seam lines are facing outwards.

2 Using a single strand of strong thread, secure the corner of a seam line with a couple of back stitches.

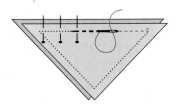

3 Sew running stitches along the marked line, working 8-10 stitches per inch (2.5cm) and ending at the opposite seam line corner with a few back stitches. When hand piecing never stitch over the seam allowances.

4 Press the seams to one side, as shown in machine piecing (Step 2).

Inset seams

In some patchwork layouts a patch will have to be sewn into an angled corner formed by the joining of two other patches. Use the following method whether you are machine or hand-piecing. Don't be intimidated – this is not hard to do once you have learned a couple of techniques. The seam is sewn from the centre outwards in two halves to ensure that no tucks appear at the centre.

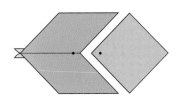

1 Mark with dots exactly where the inset will be joined and mark the seam lines on the wrong side of the fabric on the inset patch.

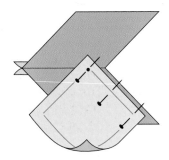

2 With right sides together and inset piece on top, pin through the dots to match the inset points. Pin the rest of the seam at right angles to the stitching line, along one edge of an adjoining patch.

3 Stitch the patch in place along the seam line starting with the needle down through the inset point dots. Secure

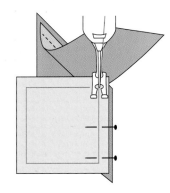

thread with a backstitch if hand-piecing, or stitch forward for a few stitches before backstitching, when machine-piecing.

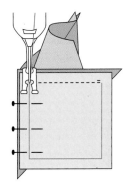

4 Pivot the patch, to enable it to align with the adjacent side of the angled corner, allowing you work on the second half of the seam. Starting with a pin at the inset point once again. Pin and stitch the second side in place, as before. Check seams and press carefully.

Working foundation-pieced Log Cabin

If you are a very experienced patchworker you will be able to do precise Log Cabin without using foundation piecing, but this is the simplest method for a novice.

1 Place the central square patch right side up in the centre of the foundation block, with each corner lined up with the diagonals (this is not so important for the free-hand blocks). Pin patch in place.

2 Position your first strip (2) over the central square patch (1), right sides together, and with the right-hand edges

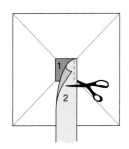

aligned. Stitch along the right-hand side to the end of the first patch, taking a ¼ in (6mm) seam allowance. Trim strip (2) evenly with the edge of patch (1), as shown. If working precise Log Cabin, press open piece (2) carefully using a dry iron. For free-hand designs, you can get away with simple finger-pressing.

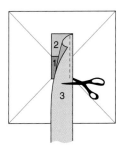

3 Turn the block anti-clockwise and lay a second strip (3) right side down over the first two pieces sewn. Stitch in place to the right-hand edge of strips (1) and (2), up to the lower edge of piece (1). Trim, and press as before.

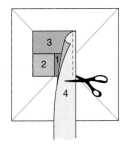

4 Turn the block anti-clockwise. Lay a third strip (4) over pieces (3) and (1). Stitch down on the right hand edge and trim evenly with piece (1). Press as before.

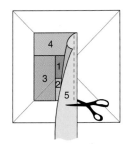

5 Turn the block anti-clockwise. Lay a fourth strip (5) over the work as before and continue in the same manner,

until you have reached the outer edges of the foundation block. **Note:** be consistent with precise foundation piecing, and always turn the block in the same direction as you add the strips, to form the blocks accurately.

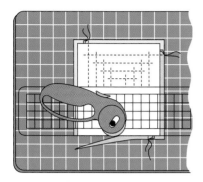

6 After the last strip has been stitched and pressed in place, it may be necessary to trim away excess fabric around the outer edge, especially with free-hand blocks. This should not really be the case for precisely pieced blocks which have been accurately cut and pieced, which should fit to the paper. To do this, use a rotary cutter and ruler, LEAVING THE DESIGNATED SEAM ALLOWANCE around the outer edge.

7 Leave the foundation papers on the blocks until they have all been stitched together to form the quilt top. Once all the blocks are joined, carefully tear away the paper backing.

Working foundation pieced Chinese Coin

1 The Chinese Coin blocks in this book are worked free-hand. Simply start by laying your first strip (1), right side up at one end of the foundation block. Pin in place.

2 Lay the second strip (2) over the first, right sides together and raw edges aligned. Taking a ¼ in (6mm) seam allowance, stitch the two pieces together. Finger-press the second strip (2) open.

3 Place a third strip (3) on top of the second strip (2), right sides together and raw edges aligned. Stitch and press as before. Continue in the same manner until the whole block is completed. Finish off as shown in steps 6 and 7 of foundation-pieced Log Cabin.

Appliqué work
Appliqué is simply a technique of stitching fabric shapes on to a fabric background to create a design. It can be applied by machine or hand using invisible blind-hem stitch or decorative embroidery stitches, such as buttonhole or satin stitch.

Machine appliqué
To make machine appliqué even easier, the fabric motifs are first fused to the base cloth with an adhesive web, which holds them in place and stops them slipping whilst they are being stitched.

1 Iron paper-backed adhesive web on to the reverse side of your appliqué fabric. If using a template, transfer the appliqué design using dressmakers' carbon paper on to the paper backing, then cut out the design. If using patterns from the fabric print itself, simply cut out the motifs.

2 Peel the paper backing off the motifs, and place them on your fabric in the desired position. Cover with a clean cloth and press motifs in place with a hot iron.

3 Using a contrasting or complimenting coloured thread, work small close zigzag stitches on your sewing machine, carefully stitching around all edges of the motif, making sure that you cover all the raw edges.

Hand appliqué
Good preparation is essential for speedy and accurate hand appliqué. The finger-pressing method is suitable for needle-turning application, used for simple shapes like leaves. Using a card template is the best method for bold simple motifs such as circles.

Finger-pressing:
1 To make your template, transfer the appliqué design on to stiff card using carbon paper, and cut out template. Trace around the outline of your appliquéd shape on to the right side of your fabric using a well sharpened pencil. Cut out shapes, adding a ¼ in (6mm) seam allowance all around by eye.

2 Hold shape right side up and fold under the seam, turning along your drawn line. Pinch to form a crease. Make sure you crease the shape so that the pencil line is just hidden at the back. Continue all round shape, snipping into the seam turnings almost to the line at any concave curves to help them turn under. Take care not to stretch the appliqué shape as you work.

Card templates:
1 Cut out appliqué shapes as shown in step 1 of finger-pressing. Make a circular template from thin cardboard, without seam allowances. You will need a separate template for each circle.

2 Using a matching thread, work a row of running stitches close to the edge of the fabric circle. Place thin cardboard template in the centre of the fabric circle on the wrong side of the fabric.

3 Carefully pull up the running stitches to gather up the edge of the fabric circle around the cardboard template. Press, so that no puckers or tucks appear on the right side. Then, carefully pop out the cardboard template without distorting the fabric shape.

Pressing stems
For straight stems, place fabric strip face down and simply press over the ¼ in (6mm) seam turning along each edge.

Needle-turning application:
1 Lay stems on to the right side of your block and tack in position down centre of stem.

2 Pin on the first leaf, right side up, tucking one end under the tacked stem. Starting close to the stem, stroke the seam allowance under with the tip of the needle as far as the creased pencil line, and hold securely in place with your thumb. Using a matching thread, bring the needle up from the back of the block into the edge of the leaf and proceed to blind-hem in place (see below). Work around the whole shape, stoking under each small section before sewing. Appliqué additional leaves in the same manner, and then the stalk in place.

3 Pin and tack flower heads to top of stems, then appliqué the flowers in place with blind-hemming stitch and a matching thread.

Blind-hem stitch

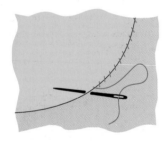

This is a stitch where the motifs appear to be held on invisibly. Bring the thread out from below through the folded edge of the motif, never on the top. The stitches must be worked small, even and close together to prevent the seam allowance from unfolding and frayed edges appearing. Try to avoid pulling the stitches too tight, as this will cause the motifs to pucker up.

Quilting and finishing

When you have finished piecing your patchwork and added any borders, press it carefully. It is now ready to be quilted and finished.

Preparing the backing and batting

- Remove the selvedges and piece together the backing fabric to form

a backing at least 3in (7.5cm) larger all round than the patchwork top. There is no need to allow quite so much around the edges when working on a smaller project, such as a baby quilt.

- For quilting choose a fairly thin batting, preferably pure cotton, to give your quilt a flat appearance. If your batting has been rolled up, unroll it and let it rest before cutting it to the same size as the backing.

Basting the layers together

1 On a bare floor or large work surface, lay out the backing with wrong side uppermost. Use weights along the edges to keep it taut.

2 Lay the batting on the backing and smooth it out gently. Next lay the patchwork top, right side up, on top of the batting and smooth gently until there are no wrinkles. Pin at the corners and at the midpoints of each side, close to the edges.

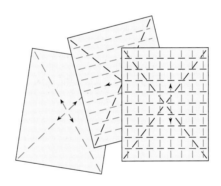

3 Beginning at the centre, baste diagonal lines outwards to the corners, making your stitches about 3in (7.5cm) long. Then, again starting at the centre, baste horizontal and vertical lines out to the edges. Continue basting until you have basted a grid of lines about 4in (10cm) apart over the entire quilt.

4 For speed, when machine quilting, some quilters prefer to baste their quilt sandwich layers together using rust-proof safety pins, spaced at 4in (10cm) intervals over the entire quilt.

Transferring quilting designs and motifs

The tool you use to mark your quilting design on to the fabric must be carefully chosen. Because of the variables of fabric in both colour, texture and fabric surface,

no one marker can be recommended. It would be a terrible shame to have made your patchwork quilt up to this stage and then spoil it with bad marking! It is therefore advisable to test out various ways of marking on scrap pieces of fabric, to test how clearly you can see the marks, and whether any lines that show after stitching can be sponged or washed away.

Chalk-based markers: these include dressmakers' chalk pencils, and powdered chalk markers. These are available in a variety of colours, and leave a clear line which often disappears during stitching or is easily removed by a brush. Chalk pencils must be kept sharpened to avoid making thick lines.

Pencils: silver and soapstone pencils available from specialist shops, both produce clear lines, which are almost invisible after quilting. Coloured pencils can be used on darker fabrics, and water-erasable ones mean the lines can be sponged away after stitching.
Pale fabrics present difficulties for marking with pencils. If you choose a lead pencil, make sure it's an 'H' type, which will leave only a fine thin line.

Perforating: the design can be transferred from a paper template on to fabric by running a tracing wheel over the outlines. With many fabrics the dotted line will last long enough for work or a portion of it to be completed.

Dressmakers' carbon paper: The carbon paper is placed working side down, between the paper template and fabric. The design can then be drawn on by tracing around the design with a pencil, or running over the design with a tracing wheel to produce a dotted line. It is available in a number of colours, for both light and dark fabrics.

Quilters' tape: a narrow re-usable sticky-backed tape, which can be placed on to the fabric surface, to provide a firm guideline for quilting straight-line patterns and grids.

Quilting through paper: some fabrics are difficult to mark for machine quilting. In these instances the design can be transferred on to tracing paper, which can be pinned to the surface of the quilt. The quilting is then done by stitching through the paper, which is then carefully torn away after quilting with the help of a blunt seam ripper.

Templates: some designs require templates, especially if a design is repeated. These can be used as an aid to help draw patterns either directly on to the quilt surface, or when drafting a design full-sized on to paper. With outline templates only the outside of the design can be drawn - any inner details will need to be filled in by hand.

Stencil templates can be made at home, by transferring the designs on to template plastic, or stiff cardboard. The design is then cut away in the form of long dashes, to act as guides for both internal and external lines. These templates are a quick method for producing an identical set of repeated designs.

Hand quilting

This is best done with the quilt mounted on a quilting frame or hoop, but as long as you have basted the quilt well, a frame is not necessary.

With the quilt top facing upwards, begin at the centre of the quilt and make even running stitches following the design. It is more important to make even stitches on both sides of the quilt than to make small ones.

Start and finish your stitching with back stitches and bury the ends of your threads in the batting.

Machine quilting

* For a flat looking quilt, always use a walking foot on your machine for straight lines, and a darning foot for free-motion quilting.

* It's best to start your quilting at the centre of the quilt and work out towards the borders, doing the straight quilting lines first (stitch-in-the-ditch) followed by the free-motion quilting.

* Make it easier for yourself by handling the quilt properly. Roll up the excess quilt neatly to fit under your sewing machine arm, and use a table, or chair to help support the weight of the quilt that hangs down the other side.

Preparing to bind the edges

Once you have quilted or tied your quilt sandwich together, remove all the basting stitches. Then, baste around the outer edge of the quilt ¼in (6mm) from the edge of the top patchwork layer. Trim the back and batting to the edge of the patchwork and straighten the edge of the patchwork if necessary.

Making the binding

1 Cut bias or straight grain strips the width required for your binding, making sure the grainline is running the correct way on your straight grain strips. Cut enough strips until you have the required length to go around the edge of your quilt.

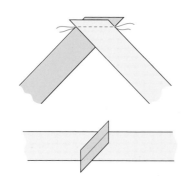

2 To join strips together, the two ends that are to be joined must be cut at a 45 degree angle, as above. Stitch right sides together, trim turnings and press seam open.

Binding the edges

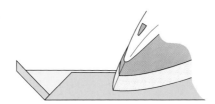

1 Cut starting end of binding strip at a 45-degree angle, fold a ¼in (6mm) turning to wrong side along cut edge and press in place. With wrong sides together, fold strip in half lengthways, keeping raw edges level, and press.

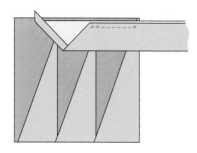

2 Starting at the centre of one of the long edges, place the doubled binding on to the right side of the quilt keeping raw edges level. Stitch the binding in place starting ¼in (6mm) in from the diagonal folded edge (see above). Reverse stitch to secure, and working ¼in (6mm) in from edge of the quilt towards first corner of quilt. Stop ¼in (6mm) in from corner and work a few reverse stitches.

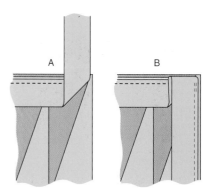

3 Fold the loose end of the binding up, making a 45-degree angle (see A). Keeping the diagonal fold in place, fold the binding back down, aligning the raw edges with the next side of the quilt. Starting at the point where the last stitch ended, stitch down the next side (see B).

4 Continue to stitch the binding in place around all the quilt edges in this way, tucking the finishing end of the binding inside the diagonal starting section (see above).

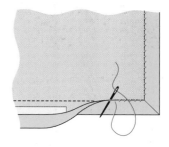

5 Turn the folded edge of the binding on to the back of the quilt. Hand stitch the folded edge in place just covering binding machine stitches, and folding a mitre at each corner.

Completing the Nine Patch Striped Bag

Note: Use a ⅜in (1cm) seam allowance throughout and stitch seams with right sides together, unless otherwise stated.

1 Stitch the plain strap sections together in pairs to form 2 pieces 30¼in (77cm) long. Repeat with the stripey strap sections. Press seams open.

2 Baste the batting pieces to the wrong side of the stripey straps. With right sides together, baste the plain straps to the stripey straps and machine-stitch straps together down the long edges. Trim seam turnings, remove tacking and turn straps through to right side. Lightly press.

3 Quilt the straps, by working 4 rows of machine stitching down the length. Place the first 2 rows ¼in (6mm) in from the edges and space the others evenly in between the first two.

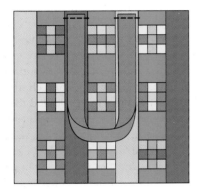

4 Baste straps in place, making sure the plain sides of the straps are facing the right side of the front and back bags, and the raw ends of each strap are level with the top edges of the 2 innermost inner borders (see diagram). Stitch in place.

5 Stitch front bag to back bag around the sides and across the lower edge. Turn bag to right side and lightly press. Stitch the bag lining pieces together around the sides and lower edge, but do not turn to right side. Press a ⅜in (1cm) hem to the inside along the top edge of the main bag and baste in place. Press a ½in (1.2cm) hem to the wrong side around the top edge of the bag lining.

6 With wrong sides together, slip the bag lining inside the main bag, making sure side seams are lined up and top edges are level. Baste bag to lining around top edge. Working close to the top edge, machine-stitch pieces together, sandwiching straps in between. Remove basting stitches.

Completing the Chequer-board Bag

Note: Use a ¼in (6mm) seam allowance throughout and stitch seams with right sides together, unless otherwise stated.

1 Stitch the strap lining sections together to form 1 piece 36½in (93cm) long. Baste the batting piece to

the wrong side of the patchwork strap. With right sides together, baste the lining to the patchwork strap and machine-stitch straps together down the long edges. Remove tacking, turn strap through to right side and lightly press. Quilt strap as shown in project on page 20.

2 Starting ¼in (6mm) up from bag base, baste and then stitch a side gusset to each side of front bag. Again starting and finishing ¼in (6mm) in from each side, attach base gusset to front bag.

3 Stitch sides to base gusset along short ends, finishing ¼in (6mm) in from the ends. Attach the bag back to the opposite edges of the gussets. Turn bag right side out and lightly press. Make up bag lining following steps 2 and 3, but do not turn to right side.

4 With right sides together and raw edges level, baste the short raw ends of the strap to the top edge of the main bag side gussets. Make sure you have not twisted the strap. Machine stitch strap in place ¼in (6mm) down from the top edge.

5 Press a ⅜in (1cm) hem to the inside along the top edge of the main bag and baste in place. Press a ½in (1.2cm) hem to the wrong side around the top edge of the bag lining.

6 With wrong sides together, slip the bag lining inside the main bag, making sure the seams all line up and top edges are level. Baste bag to lining around top edge and working close to the top edge, hand stitch pieces together with the quilting thread, sandwiching straps in between. Remove basting stitches.

Completing Blossom Bag

Note: Use a ⅜in (1cm) seam allowance throughout and stitch seams with right sides together, unless otherwise stated.

1 Press interfacing to the wrong side of the side and base gussets. Starting ⅜in (1cm) up from the bag base, stitch a side gusset to each side of the front bag. Again starting and finishing ⅜in (1cm) in from each side, attach the base gusset to the front bag.

2 Stitch side gussets to base gusset along short ends, finishing ⅜in (1cm) in from the ends. Attach the bag back to the opposite edges of the gussets. Turn bag right side out and lightly press.

3 To make up bag lining, press interfacing to the wrong side of each facing strip. Stitch a facing strip to the top edge of the front and back lining panels and 1 short end of each side gusset lining. Make up bag lining following steps 1 and 2, omitting reference to interfacing on gussets, and leaving an 8in (20cm) gap in one seam on the base gusset. Leave lining wrong side out.

4 To make handles, measure around thickness of your cord and add ¾in (2cm) to this measurement. Cut 2 bias grain strips of this width x 14in (35.5cm) long. Lay a 16in (40cm) length of narrow ribbon on top of the right side of each bias strip and stitch to one short end. Fold bias strip in half lengthways, enclosing ribbon and stitch long edges together with a ⅜in (1cm) seam allowance, taking care not to catch the ribbon into the seam as you sew. Trim the seam turnings.

5 To turn handles to right side, place the pieces of thick cord end to end with the bias strips where the ribbon is attached. Stitch ends of cord very firmly to bias strips. Then, carefully grasping the loose end of the ribbon, pull the ribbon, easing the bias strip gently down and over the cord. Continue until cord is completely covered.

6 Baste handles in place to the right side of the front and back bags, with raw ends of each handle level with top edges of bag and 3in (7.5cm) in from side seam. Stitch firmly in place.

7 Turn main bag wrong side out. Slip bag lining inside main bag, making sure the seams all line up and top edges are level. Baste bag to lining around top edge, and then stitch edges together, sandwiching handles in between. Remove basting stitches.
Turn bag to right side through gap in the lining base gusset. Slipstitch gap in lining closed.
Push lining down into bag and press the seamed top edge flat.

8 To form base stiffener, fold base strip in half lengthways and stitch long edges together. Refold strip so seam runs up the centre, then stitch across one short end. Turn through to right side. Insert cardboard stiffener, and fold raw open edges to inside. Slipstitch open edges together and drop the covered card into the bag base.

Completing the Chime Bag

Note: Use a ³⁄₈in (1cm) seam allowance throughout and stitch seams with right sides together, unless otherwise stated.

1 Stitch a bag lining to the top edge of both the decorated front and back bags, and press seams open to form 2 long rectangles with a central seam. Making sure the decorated front and back bags are facing each other and the central seams match, stitch the fronts to the backs down the 2 long edges and across the base, starting and finishing at the edges of the lining.

2 Press a ³⁄₈in (1cm) hem to the wrong side around the raw open edges of the bag lining. Turn the bag right side out and stitch the pressed open edges together. Push the lining down inside the decorated bag, and press the seamed top edge flat.

3 Press a ³⁄₈in (1cm) hem to the wrong side around each casing strip. Baste a casing strip to the right side of

both the front and back bag, placing it centrally on the bag, 2in (5cm) down from the top edge. Stitch the 2 long edges in place with a close narrow zigzag stitch over the pressed edge.

4 Cut the cord into 2 x 20in (50.5cm) lengths, and make a knot approximately 2in (5cm) from each end. Fray ends of cord beyond knot and thread a length of cord through each channel.

Completing the Cushions

Note: Use a ³⁄₈in (1cm) seam allowance throughout and stitch seams with right sides together, unless otherwise stated.

1 Press a double ¹⁄₂in (1.2cm) hem to the wrong side of 1 long edge on both large and small cushion backs, and stitch in place close to first pressed edge.

2 Place the larger back, face down, on to the right side of the cushion front with raw edge level and the hemmed edge set back from one of the front edges. Place the smaller back, face down, on top

of the uncovered side of the front cushion, keeping raw edges level and overlapping the hemmed edges.

3 Baste the cushion cover pieces together. Turn cover through to right side and insert cushion pad through centre back opening.

How to prepare a Patchwork or Quilt for hanging

To keep your patchwork flat when hanging on a wall, insert wooden dowels through channels at the top and base of the hanging. To do this, cut 2 strips of fabric 1³⁄₄in wide (4.5cm) x the width of your quilt. Press raw edges of each strip ³⁄₈in (1cm) to the wrong side, and then slipstitch the strips to the wrong side of the hanging at the top and base, along the long pressed edges. Insert ³⁄₈in- (1cm-) diameter wooden dowels cut 5cm shorter than width of quilt and slipstitch ends of channels closed.
To hang the wall hanging, stitch a brass ring to each end of top channel and use to hook them over picture hooks, or nails.

GLOSSARY OF TERMS

Appliqué The technique of stitching fabric shapes on to a background to create a design. It can be applied either by hand or machine with a decorative embroidery stitch, such as buttonhole, or satin stitch.

Backing The bottom layer of a *quilt sandwich*. It is made of fabric pieced to the size of the quilt top with the addition of about 3in (7.5cm) all around to allow for quilting take-up.

Basting Also known as tacking in Great Britain. This is a means of holding two fabric layers or the layers of a *quilt sandwich* together temporarily with large hand stitches, or pins.

Batting Also known as wadding in Great Britain. Batting is the middle layer, or *padding* in a quilt. It can be made of cotton, wool, silk or synthetic fibres.

Bias The diagonal *grain* of a fabric. This is the direction which has the most give or stretch, making it ideal for bindings, especially on curved edges.

Binding A narrow strip of fabric used to finish off the edges of quilts or projects; it can be cut on the straight *grain* of a fabric or on the *bias*.

Block A single design unit that when stitched together with other blocks creates the quilt top. It is most often a square, hexagon, or rectangle, but it can be any shape. It can be pieced or plain.

Border A frame of fabric stitched to the outer edges of the quilt top. Borders can be narrow or wide, pieced or plain. As well as making the quilt larger, they unify the overall design and draw attention to the central area.

Butted corners A corner finished by stitching *border* strips together at right angles to each other.

Chalk pencils Available in various colours, they are used for marking lines, or spots on fabric. Some pencils have a small brush attached, although marks are easily removed.

Cutting mat Designed for use with a *rotary cutter*, it is made from a special 'self-healing' material that keeps your cutting blade sharp. Cutting mats come in various sizes and are usually marked with a grid to help you line up the edges of fabric and cut out larger pieces.

Darning foot A specialist sewing machine foot that is used in *free-motion* quilting – the *feed dogs* are disengaged so that stitches can be worked in varying lengths and directions over the fabric.

Ditch quilting Also known as *quilting-in-the-ditch* or *stitch-in-the-ditch*. The quilting stitches are worked along the actual seam lines, to give a *pieced quilt* texture. This is a particularly good technique for beginners as the stitches cannot be seen – only their effect.

Dressmakers' carbon paper Also known as tracing paper. Available in a number of colours, for light or dark fabric. It can be used with pencils, or a tracing wheel to transfer a quilting design on to fabric.

Feed dogs The part of a sewing machine located within the *needle plate* which rhythmically moves up and down to help move the fabric along while sewing.

Foundation pattern A printed base exact size of a *block* onto which patchwork pieces are sewn. The foundations are usually made from soft paper, but could also be lightweight fabric, interfacing, or one of the new non-woven tear-away backings, such as *Stitch-n-tear*.

Free-motion quilting Curved wavy quilting lines stitched in a random manner. Stitching diagrams are often given for you to follow as a loose guide.

Fussy cutting This is when a template is placed on a particular motif, or stripe, to obtain interesting effects. This method is not as efficient as strip cutting, but yields very interesting results.

Grain The direction in which the threads run in a woven fabric. In a vertical direction it is called the lengthwise grain, which has very little stretch. The horizontal direction, or crosswise grain is slightly stretchy, but diagonally the fabric has a lot of stretch. This grain is called the *bias*. Wherever possible the grain of a fabric should run in the same direction on a quilt *block* and *borders*.

Inset seams, setting-in or Y-seams A patchwork technique whereby one patch (or block) is stitched into a 'V' shape formed by the joining of two other patches (or blocks).

Iron-on interfacing eg. Vilene/Pellon. A non-woven supporting material with adhesive that melts when ironed, making the interfacing adhere to the fabric.

Mitred corners A corner finished by folding and stitching binding strips at a 45-degree angle.

Needle plate The metal plate on a sewing machine, through which the needle passes via a hole to the lower part of the machine. They are often marked with lines at 1/4in (5mm) intervals, to use as stitching guides.

Padding Also known as *batting* in the United states and *wadding* in Great Britain, this is the middle layer of a *quilt sandwich*. Padding can be made of cotton, wool, silk or synthetic fibres and can be bought in sheets or as a loose stuffing.

Paper-backed adhesive web eg. Bondaweb/Wonder-Under. Can be cut to shape and pressed to the wrong side of a fabric shape using a hot iron. Then the paper backing is peeled off. The fabric shape can then be placed on top of another, adhesive side down, and pressed again to fuse in place.

Patch A small shaped piece of fabric used in the making of a *patchwork* pattern.

Patchwork The technique of stitching small pieces of fabric (*patches*) together to create a larger piece of fabric, usually forming a design.

Pieced quilt A quilt composed of *patches*.

Pins Use good quality pins. Do not use thick, burred or rusted pins which will leave holes or marks. Long pins with glass or plastic heads are easier to use when pinning through thick fabrics. Safety pins (size 2) can be used to 'pin-baste' the quilt layers together.

Quilters' tape A narrow removable masking tape. If placed lightly on fabric, it provides a firm guideline for straight-line patterns.

Quilting Traditionally done by hand with running stitches, but for speed modern quilts are often stitched by machine. The stitches are sewn through the top, *padding* and *backing* to hold the three layers together. Quilting stitches are usually worked in some form of design, but they can be random.

Quilting foot See *walking foot*.

Quilting frame A free-standing wooden frame in which the quilt layers are fixed for the entire quilting process. Provides the most even surface for quilting.

Quilting hoop Consists of two wooden circular or oval rings with a screw adjuster on the outer ring. It stabilises the quilt layers, helping to create an even tension.

Quilt sandwich Three layers of fabric: a decorative top, a middle lining or *padding* and a *backing*. Collectively known as the 'quilt sandwich'. They are held together with quilting stitches or ties.

Rotary cutter A sharp circular blade attached to a handle for quick, accurate cutting. It is a device that can be used to cut up to six layers of fabric at one time.

It needs to be used in conjunction with a 'self-healing' *cutting mat* and a thick plastic ruler.

Rotary ruler A thick, clear plastic ruler printed with lines that are exactly 1/4in (6mm) apart. Sometimes they also have diagonal lines printed on, indicating 45 and 60-degree angles. A rotary ruler is used as a guide when cutting out fabric pieces using a *rotary cutter*.

Selvedges Also known as *selvages*, these are the firmly woven edges down each side of a fabric length. Selvedges should be trimmed off before cutting out your fabric, as they are more liable to shrink when the fabric is washed. They are also difficult to quilt due to the firm nature of the weave.

Setting-in See *Inset seams*.

Stitch-in-the-ditch See *ditch quilting*.

Stitch-n-tear A new non-woven material resembling a non-woven interfacing which is used underneath fabric to support it while embroidering, or patchworking by machine. When the stitching is completed the material is simply torn away.

Staystitches Rows of directional machine stitches, placed just inside certain seamlines, to prevent them from stretching out of shape during handling and construction. The most important seamlines to staystitch are those that are curved or angled. Staystitching is done immediately before or after removing your pattern, and is worked through a single layer of fabric.

Template A pattern piece used as a guide for marking and cutting out fabric *patches*, or marking a *quilting*, or *appliqué* design. Usually made from plastic or strong card that can be reused many times.

Threads One hundred percent cotton or cotton-covered polyester is best for hand and machine piecing. Choose a colour that matches your fabric. When sewing different colours and patterns together, choose a medium to light neutral colour, such as grey or ecru. For both hand and machine *quilting* it helps to use coated or pre-waxed quilting thread, which allows the thread to glide through the quilt layers. Hand quilting can be worked in special threads, such as pearl or crochet cotton.

Tracing wheel A tool consisting of a spiked wheel attached to a handle. Used to transfer a design from paper on to fabric, by running the wheel over design lines.

Tying A quick and easy way to hold the *quilt sandwich* layers together without using machine or hand *quilting*. Thread or yarn is inserted through the quilt layers at regular intervals and tied in a knot or bow, or secured with a stitch or buttons.

Unit A small part of a patchwork design made from *patches*, which is then pieced together with other units to form a *block*.

Wadding The British term for *batting*, or *padding* (inner filling).

Walking foot Also known as a *quilting foot*, this is a sewing machine foot with dual feed control. It is very helpful when quilting, as the fabric layers are fed evenly from the top and below, reducing the risk of slippage and puckering.

Y-seams See *inset seams*.

KAFFE FASSETT FABRIC COLLECTION

See pages 73 - 76 for full range of fabric swatches

Alternate stripe
  AS10: 65
Artichokes
  GP07-C: 6, 50
  GP07-J: 40, 50, 65, 67
  GP07-L: 6, 50
  GP07-S: 6
  GP07-P: 6, 8, 26, 34
Beads
  GP04-C: 50
  GP04-J: 34, 40, 50
  GP04-L: 36, 50
  GP04-P: 6, 8, 26
  GP04-S: 36
Blue and white stripe
  BWS01: 6, 12, 16, 28
  BWS02: 28
Broad check
  BC04: 61
Broad stripe
  BS01: 65
  BS08: 40
Chard
  GP09-L: 36
  GP09-J: 40
Damask
  GP02-C: 6, 16, 26
  GP02-J: 34, 36, 40, 50, 65
  GP02-L: 6, 8, 16
  GP02-P: 8, 16, 26
  GP02-CT: 8
  GP02-S: 6
Exotic stripe
  ES04: 20
  ES20: 50
Flower lattice
  GP11-C: 36, 40
  GP11-L: 16
Forget Me Not Rose
  GP08-C: 6, 8, 16, 26
  GP08-L: 6, 8, 16, 26

GP08-J: 34, 36, 40, 50, 65
GP08-S: 6
Gazania
  GP03-C: 16
  GP03-J: 40, 50
  GP03-L: 16, 36
  GP03-P: 8, 16
  GP03-S: 6, 16, 34
Narrow check
  NC02: 40
  NC03: 40, 12
  NC05: 65
Narrow stripe
  NS01: 36
  NS09: 65
  NS17: 50
Ombre stripe
  OS01: 16, 28
  OS02: 6, 28
  OS04: 16, 28
  OS05: 28
Pachrangi stripe
  PS05: 52
  PS08: 65
  PS13: 34, 65
Pebble beach
  GP06-C: 6
  GP06-J: 26, 34, 40, 50
  GP06-L: 6
  GP06-P: 6, 8
  GP06-S: 6, 16, 26
Pressed Roses
  PR02: 28, 50
  PR04: 36, 40, 65
  PR05: 50
  PR07: 50
Roman glass
  GP01-G: 26, 34, 50
  GP01-J: 40
  GP01-L: 50
  GP01-P: 26
  GP01-R: 34, 36, 40, 50, 67
  GP01-PK: 6, 26
  GP01-BW: 6, 34, 50

Rowan stripe
  RS01: 28, 20, 23
  RS02: 28, 34
  RS03: 12
  RS04: 20, 23, 28, 46
  RS05: 8, 26, 28, 34
  RS06: 23, 28, 34
  RS07: 28
  RS08: 28
Shot cotton
  SC01: 23, 52, 56, 61, 65
  SC02: 43, 56, 61, 65, 71, 72
  SC03: 12, 43, 46, 55, 56, 58, 61
  SC04: 43, 46, 61, 65
  SC05: 23, 43, 61, 65
  SC06: 43, 46, 52, 61
  SC07: 12, 36, 52, 61, 65, 67, 71
  SC08: 12, 23, 34, 43, 52, 65
  SC09: 12, 43, 52, 61
  SC10: 34, 61, 65, 67
  SC11: 61, 65
  SC12: 12, 34, 61, 65
  SC13: 43, 61
  SC14: 12, 23, 28, 34, 43, 61
  SC15: 43, 46, 52, 61
  SC16: 34, 36, 46, 56, 61, 65
  SC17: 26, 46, 61, 65
  SC18: 46, 52, 61, 65
  SC19: 46, 50, 55, 56, 61
  SC20: 12, 23, 43, 46, 61, 52
  SC21: 12, 43, 61
  SC22: 46, 61
  SC23: 20, 23, 43, 46, 61, 65
  SC24: 23, 28, 46, 61
  SC25: 43, 46, 55, 56, 58, 61, 71
  SC26: 12, 23, 43, 61
  SC27: 12, 23, 28, 34, 36, 43, 61
  SC28: 8, 28, 67
  SC29: 20, 23, 43, 46, 55, 56, 58, 71
  SC31: 20, 43, 46, 55, 56, 58
  SC32: 43
  SC33: 20, 28, 34
  SC35: 28
  SC36: 20, 23, 26, 43

INDEX

ABBREVIATIONS

The Kaffe Fassett Fabric collection

Stripes

NS Narrow stripe
PS Pachrangi stripe
ES Exotic stripe
AS Alternate stripe
BS Broad stripe

FQ a 22½in x 20in (57cm x 50cm) piece of fabric, sold as a 'fat quarter'.

W.S wrong side.

Experience ratings

★   Easy, straightforward, suitable for a beginner.

★★   Suitable for the average patchworker and quilter.

★★★ For the more experienced patchworker and quilter.